Big government can no longer be depended upon to take care of the people during the coming collapse. The people must be freed up to do whatever it takes to survive on their own by bartering and working for each other.

It is not a history we are proud of, but right out of slavery that is how the Negro race survived in America, many black women ironed clothes and worked in white folk's homes to feed their families.

With the soon coming collapse and a broke government people will have to fiend for themselves and that can't be done unless the minimum wage is eliminated and choking regulations voided. The minimum wage and choking regulation must go, period, if this nation is to survive the soon coming collapse.

CURRENT EVENT INJECTION 19 JANUARY 2012:
KEYSTONE OIL PIPELINE DECISION!
I definitely don't need this, I would be far better off keeping my personal view to my self on this matter, but, I guess I'm a motor mouth at times and can't help it.

Anyone that has ever read any of my writing knows that I'm for small government and totally against a welfare state type government. That means that I disagree almost one hundred percent of the time with the current administrations policies. But, on this Keystone Pipeline issue I must admit that I totally agree with their decision on this.

Experts have been wrong before and will be wrong again, that is a given. Why take a chance and risk destroying the water supply of three states when it can be avoided. Sure, the cost is going to be much higher and take longer, but later saying that shouldn't have happen, or saying we are sorry won't bring back clean water.

I have personally experienced Murphy's Law in action many times. Murphy's Law says if anything bad can possibly happen it will. I think the risk is just far too great no matter what the experts say when you are talking about the water supply of three states.

To me it is a no brainier, just go around the aquifer. Sure, we are desperate in need of jobs but first we must have clean water to live.

CURRENT EVENT INJECTION 19 JANUARY 2012:
WHAT A DREAM TEAM?
Newt + JC

CURRENT EVENT INJECTION 16 JANUARY 2012!

THE CRUISE LINE INCIDENT:
MY BIGGEST SURPRISE AND MAYBE A
BIGGER QUESTION IS:
Why would a modern ship like that go down
so fast? I thought in modern ship building at
least some type of compartmentalized
structure would be in place, but, again what
do I know, maybe it is too cost prohibitive.
No matter how well trained the crew, a ship
going down
that fast with that many people there are
going to be problems.

DISSECTING USA ECONOMY
Like I've said many times, I can dissect an
economy as well as anyone.
Here is my bold brash opinion on the options
if the USA and western civilization is to
survive.

The way I see the situation in the USA is first
things first and I've yet to hear anyone hit
the target. To talk about getting out of debt
or saving our freedom while government is
still in the role of super social and family
provider in my view is dumb and stupid.

That is something that is impossible, we are
lucky that this has lasted this long. You see,
government doesn't have any money and
every penny it takes comes from some type
of business profit. The bigger government
gets the more profit it must take from

businesses until it kills off all business profit. We are not there yet, but we are headed there at warp speed.

A society must have some type of government for internal and external protection of the whole society otherwise government wouldn't be needed. Government is not part of an economy it is just a parasite needed for protection. In simple terms, an economy consists of only two players, a seller and a buyer no matter how modern or complicated it may seem.

Starting with the seller, using some form of energy the seller produces a product or service and a buyer purchases it. An employee himself is actually a seller, he sell his labor for a paycheck. A business itself is only a medium of exchange to generate a profit for the owner, if it doesn't generate a profit it can't exist.

To sum it up, government is only needed to protect society, but, it has the big guns and the power to take over and some do. And believe it or not with the course we are on that is exactly what is going to happen to the great USA, it is only logic.

Unless we start by eliminating the minimum wage and void practically all regulations the economy is guaranteed to totally collapse. After that there will be mass hunger, rioting

in the streets and a lot of people being shot, then the people themselves will demand that government take over.

However, with the eliminating of the minimum wage and choking regulations government won't collapse, but it will severely deflate and a lot of rich people will go broke. But, we will save out freedom and survive, it won't be easy but the people will regain control and the nation will survive.

Otherwise, with the course we are on freedom and the nation will be lost forever. There it is y'all all wrapped and packaged, you don't have to agree with me but that is my brief analysis.

Sure, government shouldn't be in the role of super social and family provider, but, when all else has failed government does has a responsibility to not let the poor freeze or starve. However, government also should never hand out free unearned money or food stamps to the poor or anyone else if the free market place is to survive.

The only way government can help the poor without destroying the nuclear family, the culture, and the economy is to establish government runs commissaries, housing, and clinics with the use of tokens or script for those who qualify.

Government handing out free cash and food stamps guarantees a big enough pool of paying customers where the merchant don't ever have to lower prices, thereby causing higher prices and taxes on everyone. That is what's causing this out of control consumer inflation that is killing us today.

Government can spend all it wants to and it won't cause consumer inflation unless money is handed out on an individual basis, the individual basis is what destroys the natural balance between the buyer and the seller.

I will tell any conservative, okay, you want small government, well; you can't get there from here. First, where you start is fight to eliminate the minimum wage and void countless choking regulations that will get you there, there is no other way, period. SERMONS LOG: 10 JANUARY 1727, 1005 HOURS

In sheer economic terms government as a social and family provider and having a lasting free market place at the same time simply don't mix, it is like pouring water in acid. It not only destroys a free market place economy it corrupts morals and leaves a nations culture in total ruins.

Look what the welfare state has done to the great USA, we are totally broke with trillions of dollars in debt which makes us slaves to foreign sources. And what is even scarier is we have a shallow hype prone predominate liberal news media that has left the general public totally in the dark on the true state of the nation.

With little to no nuclear and extended family foundation left and any minimum bartering capacity to sustain us under distress, this nation could become authoritarian or a dictatorship almost overnight.

In my opinion with the czars already in place and with a shallow predominate liberal news media that can't recognize a moral or deep threat if it slapped them upside the head, the only thing now saving the last bastion of true freedom in the world today is the second amendment. And its days are probably numbered.

All of which could be avoided if the minimum wage was eliminated and all big government regulations were voided and then added back as needed. We as a nation are like fools with all of our eggs still in one giant big government welfare state basket, how sad, God help us.

Around the world I imagine many are amused by the fix we are in. But, at the same time they are in almost boot shaking fear, because wise men know the most dangerous thing

there is, is when a great nation is injured or losing power.
05 JANUARY 2012, NEW INJECTION:

<u>My God! Maybe my deep wisdom is greater than even I realize.</u> A thing about the economy that seems so simple to me doesn't even register with the so called highly intelligent great economic thinkers of today.

I listen every day on this and that and what this politician is going to do to fix the economy and on and on. While at the same time welfare states all over the world is in the early stages of collapsing down upon their heads.

Still, the powers that be don't even have a clue as to the one and only thing that can save the USA and western civilization. I believe the global economy is past the stage of no return, it can't be saved, but at least western civilization itself can be saved if this one and only thing is done.

The one and only thing that I know without a shadow of doubt that will save western civilization is "Get government out of the role of social and family provider, period." However, after eighty years of ever increasing big government dependency that is an almost impossible task.

Also, another go against the grain widely held false assumption that flies in the face of sound economics is the belief that the "Minimum wage is a good thing." In economic terms the minimum wage is destructive wishful thinking, period. The minimum wage doesn't increase wealth it only distorts wealth and kills the free market place.

The minimum wage makes what cost $5.00 after awhile cost $50.00. The only thing that increases wealth is the increase in production and buying power. Without the elimination of the minimum wage it will be impossible to get the government out of its family provider role to save western civilization.

Power will always go down with the ship, only divine intervention can save us now, God help us. Government in the role of social and family provider given time will always kill an economy. It is done by taking too much profit leaving no incentive for anyone to go into or stay in business.

Given time big government will also snuff out all greed and self-interest which leaves no incentive to produce except by the whip. With the whip one will produce only enough to stay alive which is the history of communism and socialism.

So, there it is in a nut shell folks, you have the facts and a solution. You can dismiss me,

the facts, and everything else I say, but you won't prove me wrong.
SIRMANS LOG: 04 JANUARY 2012, 1220 HOURS

CURRENT EVENT INJECTION!
THE PAYROLL TAX CUT EXTENSION:
Some people are coming down hard on the house speaker saying he is a caver and can't stand up to pressure. Well, I for one totally disagree; I think he made the right decision on avoiding a tax raise on the American people.

Sure, the liberals are demagoguing the issue but that is expected and beside the point. You have a general public that is 95 percent ignorant on economic matters; they can't see past their noses and will be film flamed almost every time by the liberals, what is one to do.

With the liberals and their cohorts in the new media pouring on the demagoguery there is no doubt who will get the blame. Educating the public is the only real solution but that is no easy task after eighty years of big government liberal do-for-me entitlement propaganda.

Facing unreasonable odds a wise man will try to live to fight another day hopefully on terms more to his favor. "Fools rush in where wise

men fear to tread."
SIRMANS LOG: 24 DECEMBER 2011, 0055
HOURS

WITH NO MINIMUM WAGE THE RICH HAS
THE MOST TO LOSE THE POOR IS ALREADY
DIRT POOR!
Here is the skinny on this minimum wage
thing I keep harping on. Sure, I know almost
everybody is thinking that I'm a fool and
don't know what the hell I'm talking about,
and besides, they feel it will never happen
anyway. And they are probably right because
I have no power to make anyone do
anything.

Plus, everybody keep thinking that it don't
make sense because the poor can't make it
as is, they need to raise the minimum wage
not get rid of it. Wrong, wrong, wrong, it is
just the opposite and I so happen to be one
of the very few with the wisdom and
perspective to see it.

Without the minimum wage the welfare state
beast will get starved out of its cradle to
grave super provider role. Without
government driving up and keeping prices
high by giving money and food stamps to the
poor it would be impossible for prices to go
above what the poor can afford because there
is never enough rich to keep commerce
flowing.

Sure, government must help the very poor and not let people starve but it can be done without destroying our culture and economy like what the welfare state has done. The way you help the poor and not destroy the culture, the economy, freedom, and everything else is by establishing government run commissaries, housing, and clinics.

Plus, tokens or script must be issued to those that qualify to keep from contaminating the national free market place currency. The reason for that is there are only two players in an economy they are the seller and buyer, or the merchant and consumer.

Government was created to guard and protect the process plus the whole society. However, government has the big guns and the fighters, so, without an armed populace it is a lot easier for a tyrant to try to seize power and take over.

Through natures supreme law of "Natural selection" the buyer and seller will always keep a natural balance between the two. But, when government put in a minimum wage and all kind of regulations it destroys the balance between the buyer and the seller.

The government creates consumer inflation by giving enough buyers (poor) the money to afford super high prices. The merchant then get away with raising prices because government is paying a large enough pool to allow it, otherwise prices would have to remain lower enough for most poor folks to pay their own doctor and food bills.

Once government got a taste of being a provider it got drunk on the control and power of lording it over people. So, it decide to create the great society, food stamps and everything else from cradle to grave, no problem, just raise taxes a little higher.

While all of this was going on the rich and the very poor had it made while consumer inflation was eating the middle class alive. To tell the truth folks, I don't know how things will finally play out if the minimum is eliminated. But, I do know that if it is not eliminated we will lose our freedom and maybe even our country.

I don't have to be right and no one may agree with anything I write, still, this is the way I see it.
SIRMANS LOG: 17 DECEMBER 2011, 0014 HOURS

WHY CAN'T THE POOR CREATE SOME OF THEIR OWN JOBS?
OK, OK, I hear you America! This is what big government and the welfare state has brought us to. I think the nation is at death

door and its going to come down to first just eating and surviving. I think it is better to eat and survive than to have untold amounts of gold and riches and starve.

Once there is no threat of starving then the sky can be the limit. I'm going to go out on a limb and say something that is taboo and political incorrect way beyond measure. I'm saying there is a place for "Roles" in life provided they are not set in stone and there is freedom of choice.

Throughout history until the "New deal" and the welfare state the children, the sick, and the elderly were always taken care of in a healthy and stable environment. To me it is a given the welfare state is now collapsing down upon us I see it and know it but the egg heads and elites will never admit it until it is too late.

So, what are we going to do about being prepared when we know a change is gonna come. I think its going to come down to bare bone survival I'm here to tell you with a minimum wage in place we have absolutely no chance of surviving.

There will be millions upon million starving to death and it could take civilization back to the Stone Age. The minimum wage and government regulations are blocking anyone from bartering and surviving on their own.

No one will escape and no amount of wealth is going to get you food if no one is willing to sell. Even if you have prepared and have food it would take an army to protect you with millions starving around you.

It is simple if there was no minimum wage at least the people could barter and do for each other just to eat if nothing more. But, with a minimum wage and countless big government regulations blocking you at every turn no amount of self-initiative is gonna keep you from starving.

As it is now the welfare state as a super family provider has nearly destroyed what has guaranteed human survival for over 5,000 years, the nuclear and extended family and its "Role" system.

Sure, opportunity and freedom to all is a must and no one doubts that in this great nation. But, who is going to raise the children and care for the sick and elderly when soon our big government will be totally broke with no borrowing power.

I'm telling you its not gong to get better like the egg heads and the elites keep promising, mass starvation is on its way whether we like it
or not. I'm telling you we are about to face the sheer survival of the USA and western

civilization itself.

I feel it is my destiny at all cost to get out the stress call for this nations survival no matter my handicaps and flaws. Agree or not I feel it is a calling and duty. I fear and hate the limelight. I also feel the minimum wage is standing in the way of this nation's survival.

All praise be to God. We shall survive.
Minimum wage "I banish you" in the name of God.
SIRMANS LOG: 15 DECEMBER 2011, 0123 HOURS

SLAVERY IN ECONOMIC TERMS!
Slavery is still around in some isolated cases. When you go back in history before western civilization and private land ownership slavery played a major role in economics.

I keep telling people a free market place with free competition is the only way a nation can feed its entire people. In economic terms what freedom and the free market place actually do is release two of the most energizing forces in our human makeup.

Even today very few American understand these two forces especially liberals because on the surface they seem to go against the grain of the status quo. If you lack wisdom and perspective you won't understand these two forces which is the case with the vast majority of Americans.

The two forces I'm talking about are greed and self-interest. Like electricity these two forces are dangerous and can be deadly. The key is to harness these two powerful forces but never shut them down or hinder them too much. Only a free market place will harness this super powerful energy in a way that will produce almost unlimited abundance in everything.

Anybody following Keynesian Theory doesn't know what the hell is going on in this day and time in my view. I can dissect an economy myself, and there is no doubt in my mind the welfare state cannot and will not survive, period.

Except for a free market place economy every other economic system tends to hinder or shutoff greed and self-interest. I predict within five years the world is going to experience slavery and starving in a major way. There is nothing complicated about it, it is simply human nature at work.

No one is going to be caring and do extra work when some one else is doing less and receiving an equal reward. Sure, using fear and pain will get some production but never abundance. In this nuclear weapon age no powerful nation can get away with taking over smaller weaker nations and working them like slaves like in the distance past.

So, without a true free market place economy I will guarantee you slavery will be back with a vengeance. With no one being able to make a profit due to big government there simply will be no other way for a nation to survive. I tell it as I see it. Praise be to God, Hallelujah. SIRMANS LOG: 11 DECEMBER 2011, 12 MIDNIGHT.

PS: The biggest problem with the USA is we have gotten too far away from a true free market place economy. It is impossible to have a true free market place economy with a minimum wage in place.

UNITED STATES POST OFFICE DEBACLE?
I have my own take on the U.S. Postal Service debacle and decided to weigh in on this matter. I can only give my one man opinion on what I think is going on. It may be sort of like social security with government siphoning off money for other government spending.

My belief is some of the money that should be going to the Postal service is probably being secretly siphoned off for other government spending. Unlike most government agencies the United States Postal service is a fee for service agency.

That being the case by all means the Postal service should be able to stand on its own. I think there is a lot more going on with the Postal Service than meets the eye. The first thing is I believe there are too many cooks in the management kitchen.

The second thing is I believe politics has a strangle hold on management with no one with any real power in charge of running the place. Sure, the unions are a factor and play a major role, still, with long term low interest loans there is no logical reason why the Postal Service can't survive without all of these cutbacks.

Come on! Give me a break! Like I said, I believe somewhere money is being siphoned off and spent elsewhere in the government; however, there is no way for me to prove that.
SIRMANS LOG: 7 DECEMBER 2011, 2148 HOURS

BOLD AND IN YOUR FACE!
In my view "The Bloom is off the rose, the cat is out of the bag," the progressive liberals are throwing rocks as always but now no longer feel a need to hide their hand anymore.

We can now see from top to bottom that the progressive liberals are openly promoting the

"All for one and one for all" socialist and centralized communist like thinking. To them Individual freedom, small government, and a free market place all are seen as "The enemy of the people."

Plus, with a shallow economically ignorant predominate liberal news media riding shotgun they no longer feel a need to hide their real intent anymore. And with eighty years of false you-owe-me liberal entitlement mentality indoctrination they just may be right.

God I ask in your name, save the great USA. SIRMANS LOG: 7 DECEMBER 2011, 0951 HOURS

PS: And another thing, I think giving the military the power to arrest civilians is a first step toward taking our guns away.

Sure, the liberals played the biggest role in birthing our welfare state. But, this nation didn't get on the brink of a total economic collapse with just liberals; a lot of conservatives took the course of least resistance and looked the other way.

We know as a rule liberals are basically shallow and live in the moment, but what can be just as dangerous to freedom is a shallow conservative, especially if he wants to give arresting power to the military to arrest civilians.

JUST A LITTLE INJECTION CONCERNING "PROFIT."

I have never considered myself to be an exceptional intelligent person, still, for the life of me I can't understand why I can dissect an economy so clearly while ninety five percent of the USA population just don't get it.

To understand economics all you need to do is understand one thing and that will be ninety five percent of the battle. That one thing is profit, profit, profit, and more profit. If you don't understand what profit is you are lost and don't know what wealth is either.

I will give a quick walk through background. In the beginning before the proper tools and weapons man spent most of his awake time hunting and searching for food. There was no profit because profit is the ability to have more than you need to live on.

Once farming reach the stage to store grain and domesticate animals then profit could be realized as long as one had enough for himself and family to get through the winter. Plus, seed stock and seed grain had to be maintained, and then whatever one had over that was called profit. So, in the final analysis it will always boil down to eating or starving.

You can't eat money or any material possession. All this big government and welfare state stuff ain't gonna feed anybody if not enough people are producing food. Why go into business when all your profit goes to someone else, it's not quite there yet, but it is getting harder and harder for any business to make a profit.

That's the problem with liberals, they don't give a damn what they destroy as long as they stay in power. But, in the end there will be no power to be had because there will not be anyone making any profit for government to take and survive on
Get a grip America! One hundred years ago the only place you could find a liberal was in a rich family or maybe on a college campus. Now, the welfare state has made practical all of the poor hardcore liberals.

In over 5,000 years of written history when have the very poor ever been in favor of killing babies in the womb and men marring men, give me a break, people. And I'm supposed to be the nut case, here. I, Freddie L. Sirmans Senior will not shut up and look the other way.
SIRMANS LOG: 2 DECEMBER 2011, 2355 HOURS

IT'S TIME FOR SOME FORM OF LEGAL

PROSTITUTION TO GET CONTROL OVER PORN IF NOTHING ELSE! I HAD GRAVE RESERVATIONS ABOUT ADDING THIS ARTICLE BUT DECIDED TO DO IT ANYWAY COMES WHAT MAY. THIS IS MY ONE MANS OPINIONS ON WHY I THINK PORN IS TOTALLY OUT OF CONTROL. VERY FEW AGREE WITH ME, BUT I STAND BY MY REASONING ON THIS.

LOOK AT WHAT IS HAPPENING TO SOME OF THE SOCIAL WEBSITES AND THE PERVERTED SEXUAL SMUT THAT MANY YOUNG KIDS HAVE TO WITNESS. I'M POWERLESS TO STOP ANYTHING BUT I WANT EVERYONE TO KNOW THAT I'M MORALLY AGAINST ALL THIS MORAL ROT AND DECAY.

JUST LIKE EVERYTHING ELSE MONEY AND PAYING CUSTOMERS IS WHAT DRIVES THE PORN INDUSTRY. LOOK UP MY ARTICLE > http://flsirmans.blogspot.com/2007/08/is-illegal-prostitution-shutting-off.html SIRMANS LOG: 16 NOVEMBER 2011, 2357 HOURS

OHIO VOTE EQUALS MOB RULE ECONOMICALLY WISE!
"We have a republic if we can keep it." The founding fathers almost to a man believed that pure democracy was nothing more than mob rule, that is why we actually have a republic form of government.

The general public as a whole is almost always ignorant and uninformed on how to run a working government. It takes strong leadership that will proper educate the public and bring them along to have and keep a successful government in a free society.

Overall, I don't blame the citizens for what happened in Ohio. But, I do blame the progressive liberals that used the depression to seize the family provider role for itself and birthed the welfare state we have today. And as long as our government is in the provider role nothing or no one is going to stop it from taking the last red cent from anyone that makes a profit.

Riding shotgun for the progressive liberals is the vast predominate liberal news media which has educated to some degree 95 percent of the general public with this false welfare state you-owe-me entitlement mentality.

I'm here to tell you, you can't get blood out of a turnip meaning because of too high taxes soon no one will be able to make a profit, then guess what, there will be no one making any profit for government to take in the form of taxes. Then a broke government ain't gonna be taking care of anyone. The people are supposed to be taking care of the government not the government taking care of the people in the first place.

The nuclear and extended family system have never failed to guarantee human survival in well over 5,000 years. But, here we are with our dumb asses putting all of our faith in a welfare state beast that dies with a broke government. And there has never been and never will be a government that doesn't go broke at some point. Also, according to the supreme law of nature when you take away the survival need for anything you make it extinct in time.

With the welfare state that is what we are doing to the nuclear and extended family system by slowly making it extinct. There must be a divine reason why a neurotic handicap like me came out of the woodworks to bring back some sanity before all of this shallow dumb insane thinking takes this great nation over a cliff.

Sure, the Ohio voters won their public employees union battle, but that will demand higher taxes. The unions may have won that battle but the whole state will loose the war when people begin starving.

When you kill the goose that lays the golden egg of profit with the scatter gun of higher and higher taxes, mass starvation always follow. Nature's supreme law of "Natural selection" guarantees that. And the reason we have never ending higher and higher taxes is because government is a family provider.

Sure, veteran and a few other pensioners is a good thing, but government should never become a mass family provider if it is to survive long term, because like any broke and desperate family provider it's going to lie, beg, borrow, or steal to feed its dependents. So, if you think our soon to be broke provider welfare state won't do something terrible and unimaginable you are fooling yourself.

However, government does have a duty as a last resort to make sure the poor and needy doesn't freeze or starve. But, the only way the government can help the poor and needy without destroying the free market place economy is to establish government run commissaries, housing, and clinics. And token or script must be used to prevent contamination of the nations currency.

Government should never under any condition give out free money or food stamps on an individual basis. The key is "Individual basis," because that act alone is what ignites consumer inflation by creating a bigger enough pool to allow high priced merchants to never have to lower their prices in order to stay in business.

That causes everyone to pay higher and higher prices and taxes in a never ending upward spiral, and it also destroys the buying power of the dollar in the process. No matter what the learned egg heads and elites may tell you, "I" say nothing else can ignite and driver consumer inflation out of sight like what is happening now, I double dog dare you, prove me wrong.

See my emergency USA survival blueprint > http://www.flsirmans. com/FLSirmansEmergencyUSAsurvivalBluePrint
SIRMANS LOG: 9 NOVEMBER 2011, 1815 HOURS

THE PHENOMENON OF "HERMAN CAIN" AS SEEN BY SELF-MADE WRITER FREDDIE L. SIRMANS, SR.
They say that life is a cycle and history repeats itself. And in this case we may again have two great African American men squaring off to shape the course of history, but in this case it is not about their race but the direction of the whole nation.

In the first case it was William E. B. Du Bois versus Booker T. Washington on which course the African American race would take. Washington believed that African Americans should take the self reliance route and focus first on learning the basic trade vocations to feed and control their own destiny.

He didn't put a priority on integration. On the other hand, Du bois disagreed openly in public with Washington and believed that African Americans should not be limited in anyway. Du bois believed that blacks should go the full integration route and focus on the best education possibly.

Du bois way won out on the course blacks should take. Sure, overall Du Bois way did win out in theory but it have never paned out in practice even to this day in my view.

However, this time around so much about America has greatly changed; African Americans are no longer the largest minority group anymore. Plus, in my view the ideology factor is even more the deciding factor than the race factor except for the fewer and fewer secret raciest.

In my view and backed by what I seen on a call in TV show, most of the most vicious attacks on Cain came from African American callers, even one black lady called him a monkey. Coming out of slavery and even to this day I don't think most African Americans have unconditional accepted a black identity.

I think still far too many African Americans see other blacks as competitors and in some cases the enemy instead of an honorable fellow independent authority figure. Why else would so many of us use the hated "N" word in private if not in public as if it doesn't apply to each of us personally.

I think the welfare state has locked most African Americans into a do-for-me dependent mode. I think one political party practical own the African American race, and that could never happen to a people that individually think for themselves.

That said, enough of me putting down my proud African American race. No one, no race, and no nation is perfect. When all is said and done, overall I truly believe the African American race to be one of the greatest people to ever exist. Sure, I may criticize and come down hard, but to me it is constructive criticism and done out of genuine love.

Against overwhelming odds and stripped of their culture, language, and religion these people withstood slavery and came out illiterate in a hostile environment with almost nothing. They didn't have the option to escape and blend in because of their color.

Still, they created Jazz, and have made great achievements in every phase of American life, they are survivors. And today we see a man of color in the White house, and even greater is a country that have allow this unlimited freedom to happen.

At heart I'm a conservative, but in practice I behave more as a pragmatist or realist. A black conservative to a liberal is like someone shelving a Christian cross in the face of vampire. They screech and see it as a threat to their very being, and that same reaction also applies to the hordes of dependents depending on the liberals to stay in power.

The mass liberal media will never accept a genuine African American conservative in my view. They just can't understand why a black person in their view can reject their helpful do-good intentions. You see, it is all about control to them, a liberal loves controlling more than anything else because that adds a purpose to their life.

A self-sufficient do-for-yourself conservative black threatens the whole welfare state reason for being, and to a liberal there is no greater sin. To them he must be destroyed at all cost.

Which way will the nation go? Will it zoom warp speed into a failed socialist European like system or take the small government free market place course as the founding fathers designed the country to be, your vote matters, the future is in our hands.

PS: 2 NOVEMBER 2011, 0106 HOURS: BRIEF

INJECTION:
I may be wrong on this, but if anything can pry the 90 percent plus loose this may be it the way the vicious partisan liberal media are going after this decent high moral black man.
SIRMANS LOG: 30 OCTOBER 2011, 1343 HOURS

SIRMANS LOG: 4 DECEMBER 2011, 1745 HOURS
Well, Herman Cain decided to throw in the towel, who can blame him. That means there won't be a showdown between two men of color for the president of the United States.

I think Dick Nixon said it best when he said "You won't have Richard Nixon to kick around anymore." Well, in my view the bias predominate liberal news media won't have "Ole Herman" to kick around anymore.

PS: Here is the reason for the 90 percent plus African American voting for one political party in every election in my view.

I DON'T KNOW WHEN, BUT I KNOW THE USA ECONOMY IS GOING TO COLLAPSE. I AM SO PROUD TO BE AN AMERICAN, FOR SOME STRANGE REASON I JUST FELT A NEED TO SAY THAT.

When I promise you the USA economy is going to collapse it really is a no brainier because it is the same as saying everybody is going to die. I understand it but the egg heads and the elites have tunnel vision and don't understand the role nature plays in economics.

Mother natures supreme law of "Natural selection" controls economics and everything else that exist. According to the law of natural selection there must be a survival need for anything to continue to exist, otherwise nature starts getting rid of it.

There is no survival need for moral decay and inefficiency, so it gotta go and if it means taking down a nation, too bad. Everything erodes or decays in some way and that includes ideas. Look at the great USA; it is now weighted down with moral decay, big government waste and inefficiency.

But, big government is much too powerful and will never allow small correcting purges that would cause much hardship but save the national economy. That is why nature's law of natural selection has no choice but to take down the nation's economy and maybe the whole world economy.

However, nothing in the future is ever written in stone man through his actions always has the power to determine his destiny. Throughout history there has never been a nation that changed course knowing it was headed toward disaster.

The reason is power never willingly concedes an inch, those wielding power will always go down with the ship. Due to the Rosetta stone we know that a written history and civilization goes back well over 5,000 years. The Roman Empire lasted a thousand years.

Ever since the dawn of history governments and rulers have always come and go, but, there was three constants over time that always stood firm until the "New deal" birthed the welfare state. Now, the whole of western civilization is on the ropes and may not survive all due to the infestation of the welfare state.

The three constants I'm talking about are the three pillars that allows human civilization to exist in my view: (1) A strong nuclear and extended family system, (2) a strong moral and religious code, (3) and adequate emergency bartering capacity with many, many small farmer and home gardeners in case the economy collapses.

Since the "New deal" birthed our welfare state we now depend almost entirely on our super provider welfare state from cradle to grave. Neglecting and dismissing the things that has safeguarded civilization for over 5,000 years to me is pass dumb and stupid, it is sheer madness. God forgive us. SIRMANS LOG: 24 OCTOBER 2011, 2247 HOURS.

MY ANALYSIS ON WALL STREET OCCUPIERS! I believe what you see being played out with the Wall Street occupiers is a microcosmic example of what is being learned on the nation's universities and college's campuses.

I think almost 95 percent of the American people to some extent have bought into the liberal welfare state entitlement mentality. They call it the safety net and feeding the welfare state beast must be done to protect that at all cost.

This nation has been around 235 years and has always had to struggle with financial ups and downs but it was always armed with a strong nuclear and extended family system along with a good moral and religious code in place.

Starting with the "New deal" that birthed our welfare state we no longer have these solid foundation building blocks to withstand an all out struggle to survive as a free nation any more. Sure, we can keep feeding our tax hungry welfare state beast a little longer to buy time, but unless my blue print survival plan is taken seriously I see very little hope. See my emergency USA survival blueprint > http://www. flsirmans.com/FLSirmansEmergencyUSAsurvi valBluePrint

I believe what you see with the Wall Street occupiers are people with very weak survival instincts that have bought the liberal claptrap welfare state entitlement mentality lock stock and barrel. They don't care or even realize that with very few exceptions the rich got their money the hard way, they worked for it and made great sacrifices.

They don't realize that job don't just drop out of heaven. They don't realize that jobs are created by people just like you and I that didn't sit around waiting on someone else to act. These people took great financial risk and in most cases fought against great odds to provide a job for themselves and many, many others.

These people are our job providers and should be praised. And anyone attacking them is either ignorant or stupid in my view. Even the definition of what a job is has been distorted. Everybody is all hung up on thinking that a job must come with health and pension benefits, nonsense, that is something that started with our welfare state.

Sure, to get that is great but to get any job to survive should be the first priority. Myself,

I blame everything that is causing our downfall on our welfare state. Today even someone with self-initiative have a mountain to climb because of all kind of government licenses and permits.

It is getting to where it is almost impossible for some one to start small. Starting small is what made America great? The old saying "Living of the land doesn't apply anymore. I don't know where it is all going to end, but, I do know without a doubt that our welfare state cannot and will not survive. God save America.
SIRMANS LOG: 23 OCTOBER 2011, 0104 HOURS

PS: And here is another thing I decided to comment on. But, let me say this first, I seldom comment on any politician or any individual. Here goes my take on governor Perry, I don't care what anyone says I believe it is what he said about social security that have hurt his chances to be president.

I, and many, many others totally agree that what he said was factual true, but we are not trying to become president of the united states. I remember when he first entered the race and zoomed right to the top. I, like most Americans knew only that he was a very successful Texas governor.

I have heard the old folks mention first

impressions many times, but even now I never get carried away on something like that, the same as judging a book by the cover, but I guess in some cases it really does matter.

Right after he called social security a ponzi scheme I thought to myself, wow, does he know the old folks are the biggest and most powerful voting block in the country, and social security is like a God to them? So, in my view that statement was like spotting your opponent twenty paces from git go.

Sure, the pundits will be all over the map with all kinds of reasons why he can't get a leg up, but I believe unless he can find a way to defuse that social security statement nothing is going to work. There is no running away from it he must go for an all out repent of his sin and ask for complete forgiveness for speaking ill will against social security.

He must promise to never attack or speak ill will of social security ever again. Nothing short of getting the old folks to forgive him of his past social security beliefs are going to allow him to become president of these United States in my view.

There is no shame in just saying I was just plain wrong about social security, the old folks are a caring and forgiving people.

Besides, there was one powerful bible character that spent years putting down Christianity but ended up being one of its greatest protectors.

I, Freddie L. Sirmans, Sr. I am a self-made writer that write what I truly think and believe, I could be wrong on this but that is my analysis.

EVERYBODY IS ALREADY PAYING TOO MUCH TAX, AND DEMONIZING THE RICH IS STUPID IN MY VIEW!
I found myself smiling while listening to a liberal lion go on and on about the rich not paying their fair share of taxes and blaming everything on the republicans.

Whereas, I know beyond a shadow of a doubt that it is the liberals claptrap garbage mentality that have brought this great country almost to its knees with this welfare state beast Lording it over all of us. The reason why I couldn't help but smile is because sometimes humor is the best way to defuse and accept a sad situation.

As I sat listening to this super liberal lion spout on and on the standard liberal blame shifting garbage it made me feel so befuddled

and sad knowing nearly half of the nation is flimflammed by this stuff. I'm afraid it may be too late now history and our destruction is on the liberals side unless a miracle take place, its going to take some hard decisions and
hardship to save this nation and I'm not for sure we have the stomach
for it.

I am almost alone yelling and hollering to deaf ears, no one want to hear me, when I yell get rid of the minimum wage and never give anyone money or food stamps on an individual basis, they think my God give wisdom is stupid. Still, I will never loose hope and stop trying to help save this great nation.

Like I have said many times before when it becomes almost totally acceptable to attack the rich, freedom and democracy is on its last leg, and I condemn anyone that does it. When you see entertainers, sport figures, business executives and others making extreme amounts of money that is because of big government and our welfare state, don't blame these people more power to them.

In a free market place economy with unhindered competition no extremes can get out of hand, only government can get between the merchant and the consumer and ignite consumer inflation by subsiding higher and higher prices enabling enough people to pay them. There never has been and never will be a rich and prosperous country without a lot of rich people to make it happen.

Poor people with money are not the same as rich people, there is a world of difference in mentality, plus almost all rich people have a strong sense of altruism, which is not the case with most of the very, very poor.
It may not seem so, but if you scratch below the surface of most genuine failures in life you will find a very self centered individual.

Without exceptions trying to make everyone equal in life will always make everyone equally poor except a very few privileged leaders. Look at history, the first thing every dictator or any power grabber does is go after and attack the rich, because they know the rich is the lifeblood of every democracy.

In a democracy the loyalty of the rich is a must because if the rich can't keep and hold on to their money they have the means to leave. I believe turning people against the rich is one of the most destructive things you can do to a free and democratic country. The old saying "Ways and actions speak louder than words" should wake people up but it doesn't.

Myself, I have been out here for years beating the bushes trying to drive the political snakes out into the opening, but to little or no avail. I think the liberals really mean well but human beings and what motivates them is something they have never understood.

Liberals just don't care or understand that when you do for and make a human being a dependent you destroy that persons will to survive on his own. Balance is the real key to human survival, to little struggle to survive can be as bad as too much hardship to survive.

One reason why we may loose our freedom is our lack of instilling good judgment and character in our young. I believe good sound judgment and character can only be instilled with a certain amount of real or imposed hardship and struggle. I'm not in favor of any harsh extreme hazing, but the idea comes from imposing some form of hardship to help build character.

Sure, many will disagree with me on the necessity of hardship and struggle to build character; still I stand my ground on this. Why do you think drug use is so out of control in this country, character may not be the main factor but it definitely plays a role?

The struggle to survive in all species have evolved over thousands of
years and when struggle is taken away life tends to become less

appreciated and leaves an unfulfilled void. To a large extent that is what has happen to this great country, far too many people today have weak survival instincts.

Far too many people couldn't recognize a moral threat if it slapped them upside the head. Far too many feel, who care if a man marries a man or a woman, marries a woman. Far too many feel it is only a fetus, who cares; the welfare state is going to take care of me in my old age.

What they don't know is nothing or no one escapes nature's supreme law of "Natural selection" but only so long. Nature's supreme law of natural selection purges out moral decay, inefficiency, and waste through births and rebirths.

The world is entering the early stage of a rebirth, and I'm here to tell you any nation without a strong nuclear and extended family system, a strong moral and religious code, and some bartering capacity with small farmers and home gardeners will have little or no chance of surviving.
SIRMANS LOG: 17 OCTOBER 2011, 2045 HOURS.

EMERGENCY USA SURVIVAL BLUE PRINT.
I stump my shoe hard on the wood floor and slam my hat down on the floor, too! And

think, damn, damn, damn! Can't somebody
understand simple logic! I'm no genus, what I
keep telling people is just simple logic,
whatever happened to people with even a
little perspective! Have the welfare state
destroyed even that!

Here it is again in a nut shell, I'm talking
about the core problem, the root problem,
the heart of the matter, the eye of the storm
or whatever you call it. No amount of money
or anything you do is going to save the USA
and our freedom as long as we have a super
family provider welfare state beast in control.

Nothing and I mean nothing as long as
government is giving out money and food
stamps on an individual basis is going to save
our economy simply because that act alone
kills the free market and drives inflation.
So, until the government is out of the family
provider role 9-9-9 or any revenue raising or
anything else is going to saving our great
nation.

A provider welfare state is like a giant
snowball rolling down hill, nothing is going to
stop it. The more it takes in taxes the more
it's going
to need to feed its growing list of dependents,
it feeds on itself, the
more it grows the more it demands in never
ending new taxes. Look what it has already
done to the great USA, It has already almost

totally destroyed the African American nuclear family and the rest of the country is not too far behind.

It has ripped our morals to threads where the word marriage now means anything one want it to. And our culture has come to mean me first, I want mine, I want it all, and on and on it goes. With a provider welfare state more money simply means giving it more power to grow.

Feeding our welfare state beast is the root cause of jobs going overseas and the other stupid things that is happening today. Behind it all in truth is the liberal's blind insane need to keep our provider welfare state beast as their Lord and Master. Whether we admit it or not we all are slaves to this beast. I rest my case, there is no reason to go on and on, if you don't get the point by now you never will.

Here is my blue print, Congress and the President must first, completely get rid of the minimum wage. Next, void all regulations on businesses, and then add them back as needed. Next, establish government run commissaries, housing, and clinics and use token or script to prevent contaminating the nations free market economy. And finally, government must stop giving out free money and food stamps to anyone on an individual basis because that is what causes consume inflation and destroys the free market.

Also, all government spending and burdens should be limited to defense, treasure, state, interior, and only what the people can't do for themselves and collect taxes accordingly. In closing I suggest this blue print be taken seriously as a guide only. I am only trailblazing a path, with that I have done my duty.

I have no father control, may God bless this great nation. I am under no illusions, I know this blue print will be totally ignored; one reason is because U.S. Senators are no longer appointed by their states and the people are no longer the sole family providers. In reality whoever is the family providers actually rules and controls the country, it's just that simple in a free republic like ours. Cry me a river.

Now, in truth the welfare state has almost all of the real power. The states and the people can piss and moan and bitch all day long, but that's about all in terms of making real changes. Instead of the United States senators being controlled by their state governor and congressmen they owe their real loyalty to special interest. And the people owe their real loyalty to who pays them, which is our welfare state with fewer and fewer exceptions.
SIRMANS LOG: 5 OCTOBER 2011, 1632 HOURS

9 OCTOBER 2011, 0844 HOURS, THIS INJECTION:
According to the U.S. constitution the military and protecting the nation is the first duty and priority of congress and the president. But, here we are today with a congress avoiding its duty by assigning it to a committee of six with OUR NATION SAVING military's neck on the chopping block.

In my one man's opinion that is a crying shame. My advice to congress is to take my advice and vote to eliminate the minimum wage right now, not tomorrow. That will get the ball rolling on saving our economy and the nation, God bless and keep a free America.

The constitution was originally designed for senators to represent the interest of their state government no one else's. That was the reason they were appointed instead of elected in the first place.

STIMULUS, STIMULUS, DUMB, DUMB, I THINK!
To me a stimulus package is like putting paper money down a rat hole. All it does is make a bad situation worse. When a nation is spending almost twice as much as it is taking in it is insane to think more spending is the

answer, it is impossible to spend your way out of debt.

I truly understand how an economy works and to me the answer is very simple. The first truth is government spending is the problem and until that is recognized and admitted there is no saving the USA and global economy. What congress and the president need to do first right now is recognize that this nation's survival is at stake and act accordingly.

Instead of going on silly financial wild goose chases, void all regulations on businesses right now. Next, completely eliminate the minimum wage. Next, set up temporary emergency government run commissaries, government run housing in all these empty buildings, government run clinics, and use tokens or script for all who qualify for these government services.

Next, stop all government spending except for military and essential government only functions. I know to most this line of thinking will be seen as insane, but, I assure you the stimulus path will lead to guaranteed doom for the USA, or we end up as a debt slave owned and controlled by foreigners.

My way to salvation is only a suggested path to take it doesn't have be word for word like I say but the path is a way out of no way, a word to the wise should be sufficient. God bless America.

PS: This path will set the USA economy free and guarantee without a shadow of doubt that entrepreneurs and the free market will save this great nation with freedom intact, nothing else can do that.

We must place all of our faith and trust in the proven ideology of the "Free market place at work.
SIRMANS LOG: 1 SEPTEMBER 2011, 0846 HOURS

IS HURRICANES THE WRATH OF AN ANGRY GOD?
The ancients certainly thought so and came up with human sacrifices and all kinds of appeasements. Believe it or not, however, excluding the sacrifices there are still some that fall prey to that type of thinking.

Myself, to that type of thinking I say poppycock, hogwash, bullcrap, or some other tits on a boar hog like metaphor. It is all nonsense, what goes around comes around and that includes the works of Mother Nature. It also includes the working of every economy, too.

Every economy has a boon and bust cycle

and sooner or later the bust cycle is going to come back around no matter how much scheming and fine tuning the egg heads does. That is just a fact of life.

So, when we become dumb and stupid and let the welfare state replace and destroy our bread and butter nuclear and extended family system that leaves us up S... Creek without a paddle.

Today when most people first read my writing they think I must be some kind of extreme right wing kook or loon that is out of touch. What they don't realize is one hundred years or so ago 95 percent of Americans though as I do.

The validity of a strong nuclear and extended family system with good morals and values haven't changed in five thousand years; it is we who have changed for the worst as a people since the "New deal" birthed our welfare state.

When the wood chopper gave up on trying to splitting a mighty oak block before walking away he decided to knee down and takes a closer look. And sure enough he could barely see it but there was a tiny beginning split. He realized all of his long hard effort had not been totally wasted.

I feel the same as the great wood chopper,

except after all these years of my writing effort I still can't see any reward, I wish I could just quit and walk away and never look back, but, I know I must carry on as long as any life left in me. I guess if I can enlighten just one person it will
have been worth it.
SIRMANS LOG: 30 AUGUST 2011, 1135 HOURS.

OMG! JUST WHAT I NEED! THE IRS!
I placed all of my faith in Turbotax for the last few filing years. Now, here comes the IRS hot on my tail and
closing in fast. Hopefully, I will
live and survive to write another day.

I'm not complaining I'm a big boy now, I can take it; I just hope I
escape with my hide and not be skinned alive. Seriously, if its determine that I owe I will pay, I may be too proud to beg but I'm not too proud to pay. I have active duty served my country and will always gladly do my citizens duty.

As a writer, maybe some humor can be found here; I have shared so much about my life, why close my life book on this. God bless and keep this great nation always.
SIRMANS LOG: 23 AUGUST 2011, 1806 HOURS.

GOD BLESS OUR FEDERAL RESERVE!
This idea of getting rid of the Federal Reserve is just plain dumb and stupid. That is like saying get rid of the government. You can't have an organized society without government.

There must be a government to protect and safeguard the whole society. However, what I am against is a welfare state type of government, which I believe is unconstitutional. Without government means anarchy with every man for himself.

The same thing applies to the economy; there must be some type of organized money system. Otherwise, you are left with only trade and bartering to survive. These people talking about getting rid of the Federal Reserve are just plain ignorant, it is the best organized money system known to man.

What type of currency to use is left up to congress and the president? Maybe it's time congress and the president considers getting back to a genuine physical currency with its value in the currency itself. But, to seriously consider getting rid of the Federal Reserve is shallow and short sighted.

What are you going to replace it with, a feudal system with Lords and castles, I think not. Right or wrong that is my one man's

opinion.
SIRMANS LOG: 21 AUGUST 2011, 0730
HOURS

FOOD STAMP'S DESTRUCTIVE POWER!

I place food stamps as the third most destructive force behind the "New deal" and the minimum wage to a genuine free market place economy.

Number one is the "New deal" when it started giving free unearned money to the poor. Sure, the poor must be helped as a last resort and not allowed to starve. But, if the free market place is to survive the government must never give out free unearned money to anyone.

The only way the government can help the poor and disadvantage without destroying the free market place is by temporary establishing government run commissaries, housing, and clinics. And even that should be done only as a last resort after the extended family, the church, the community, and all else has failed.

Otherwise a survival need for the nuclear and extended family will be replaced by government and in time the nuclear family will cease to exist. The reason why that will in time kill every economy is because there are only two players in an economy; they are a seller and a buyer or merchant and consumer.

The government is only a necessary parasite needed to protect the whole society. Government has the power and the big guns and many times takes over and run the whole show, but only a free market place economy can feed its entire population.

In a free country if government would just stay with collecting taxes, protecting the country, and doing only what the people can't do for themselves the economy would police itself and produce far more than the population could use.

Mother Nature's supreme law of "Natural selection" would maintain a natural balance between the buyers and sellers and purge out inefficiency, moral decay and other anti-survival forces. But, when government takes its tax money and gives out on individual basis free unearned money and food stamps to the poor that creates enough people with the money to keep higher and higher priced merchants in business.

Then the government raises the taxes on the higher and higher priced merchants and the merchants pass their extra cost on to the public in a never ending inflationary spiral. After the "New deal" and the government started giving out free unearned money on an individual basis that ignited inflation but by then government had tasted the God like power of being a super provider.

Then the die was cast and I don't believe big government ever intend to give up one inch of its cradle to grave God like great white father provider role come hell or high waters. When it comes to money it is not the amount that truly matters it is the buying power that really counts.

Once inflation kicks in higher taxes on merchants only means higher prices passed on to the public. I didn't research when the minimum wage was started but at some point government decided the minimum was a good idea, I totally disagree.

All the minimum wage does is remove the safety valve from a free market place economy, it is then like a vehicle with no reverse or a hot water heater with no pop off valve. Folks, now don't get me all twisted I know the things I criticize was genuine intended to help the poor and to a lesser extent get politicians elected.

I know food stamps was meant to be a good thing but just like free unearned cash it is deadly destructive to a free market place economy when given out on an individual basis.

With government not giving out free money to the poor It is impossible for most merchants to charge more than the poor can pay and stay in business because there is never enough rich to keep commerce flowing. When government is not involved in the free market place that will keep the cost of living down to where the people can pay their on food and doctor bills.

When government do help the poor and disadvantage by establishing government run commissaries, housing, and clinics it should always use tokens or scripts. That will make sure government spending is kept separate and not contaminate the nation's economy in any way.
SIRMANS LOG: 17 AUGUST 2011, 1245 HOURS.

LAST CALL TO ELIMINATE THE MINIMUM WAGE!
The egg heads, the ruling class, and the elites all think I'm some kind of nut case that few knows about and I should be ignored out of existence, wrong.

When I keep harping on completely eliminating the minimum wage they think I'm a fool and don't know what I am talking about, wrong, Eliminating the minimum wage is the only thing that is going to save western civilization by starving the welfare state beast out of its all powerful super provider role.

That and that alone can set the free market place free to save western civilization. Nothing else can do it. That act alone will permit the nuclear and extended family system to rebound along with good moral and plenty of emergency life sustaining bartering capacity. Otherwise, if we fail to eliminate the minimum wage western civilization is done.

It will very soon have zero chance of surviving. The reason is Mother Nature herself is going to use its supreme law of "Natural selection" to reset western civilization back to zero, in other words the Stone Age.

The welfare state has destroyed 90 percent of the foundation that holds every society together. And without the elimination of the minimum wage the welfare state will complete the job with 100 percent destruction. I'm talking about a 100 percent destruction of the nuclear and extended family system.

As to good ethics and morals, right now we have men marring men and women marring women and before long good ethics and morals will be something found only in the history books. And the old standby of having adequate emergency backup bartering capacity in case the economy fails, meaning many, many small farmers and home gardeners, they are now like so many, sucking on the welfare state provider tit.

Just in case anyone is thinking that if things get out of hand martial law will be used to demand order by force, could be in for a rude awakening. At this point western civilization without eliminating the minimum wage soon won't have any foundation left to support civilization or an organized society.

That being the case no amount of authority can prevent total chaos back to the Stone Age. Only the elimination of the minimum wage can save what little that is left of a foundation to survive on and reverse course before going over the cliff and taking western civilization with it.

Of course, I know I will be ignored more than ever but I believe my great supernatural wisdom is God given. Go ahead a laugh and dismiss me as a bigger nut than ever, but, one thing is for sure "We all dance to the tune of a distance drummer." Glory be to God.

The real secret is, life is all about maintaining a balance, and I know most of my views are too one sided and to the extreme, but only drastic thinking and actions at this late stage can create a middle balance.

Once the minimum wage is eliminated the next step is the government must never give out free money to help anyone on an individual basis. To help the poor, needy or anyone the government must establish temporary commissaries, housing, and clinics and use tokens or script for those that qualify.

That will prevent government spending from igniting inflation and destroying the free marking place like what is killing today's economy. I assure you sooner or later some nation is going to see the light and grab my no minimum wage lifeline wisdom, not every one is going to play Russian roulette with their nations' survival.
SIRMANS LOG: 07 AUGUST 2011, 0011 HOURS

"OOPS! THERE IT IS!"
Like I've said before, the liberals will see you in hell before they will cut spending and stop the growth of government. For whatever reasons, those pushing for the collapse of the USA and global economies, it may be all down hill from here.

I knew it, I knew it, the conservatives and others would not be able to withstand the pressure, now I guarantee you taxes are going to be raised on the fewer and fewer businesses left standing. Lord knows I hope I'm wrong on this, but I'm afraid this may be the final nail in the coffin before the sunsets of the USA and global economies.

Like a broken record I'm still at it on pleading for the eliminating of the minimum wage. I yell to the world this welfare state beast is out of control and is just too powerful and mighty. But like David with his stone and sling shot I promise you, the elimination of the "Minimum wage will bring this beast to its knees and put the people back in control over their government.

Nothing else is going to break its death grip on the USA and global economies. The dam is about to burst, and once the dominos start falling no one knows where it's going to end, it may be back to the Stone Age, and only God knows, God save America, Amen.
SIRMANS LOG: 02 AUGUST 2011, 1455 HOURS

THE FORGOTTEN, ONLY GUARANTEED PENSION!
What this entitlement generation has forgotten or don't even know is for over 5000 years your only survival pension was your children.

Until around eighty years ago when the "New deal" and this monster size welfare state came about the nuclear and extended family system allowed civilization to exist for over 5000 years. It is not a perfect system but no society have ever survived and existed without it in the history of man kind.

In the USA except for maybe a few veterans almost no one was on the government dole before the "New deal" came along. Sure, in the beginning social security was a good thing for the elderly and the severely disadvantaged, but now every body and his brother is on it.

Those that put all of their faith in government don't know history, there has never been a government that didn't go broke at some point. To let this big government welfare state kill the nuclear family system by taking away it survival need like what is happening is not only dumb and stupid it is sheer madness.

Never put all of your survival eggs in one basket, especially a tax hungry out of control welfare state beast. The biggest problem now is the welfare state has produced so many dependents so long that nearly 40 percent of the population has no clue as how to survive using self-initiative.

I wish somebody would please show me how in the hell you are going to pay your way out of debt by going deeper into debt, like the

liberals are trying to do.
SIRMANS LOG: 30 JULY 2011, 2025 HOURS.

MASS ECONOMIC IGNORANCE!
About 95 percent of the American people's knowledge of how an economy truly works can be compared to a little kid that believes grits and eggs come only from the grocery store.

Even most economist has bought into this liberal garbage claptrap entitlement mentality that started with the "New deal." But, I'm here to tell you there are no free rides in life somebody always pays.

All wealth originates from some type of trade or business transaction by the private sector, period. No wealth originates from government it is always taken from somebody or somewhere. The first rule in economic is "You can't get blood out of a turnip."

You can't eat money and if there are not enough people producing food there is going to be starvation no matter who the liberals blame. When a nation prevents the private sector from making a profit it cuts its own throat that is biting the hand that feeds it.

Only a free market place nation can create wealth and feed its entire people, all other

economic systems leads to mass starvation, that is the history, you can look it up. But, when have a liberal ever had common sense, very seldom in my view.
SIRMANS LOG: 29 JULY 2011, 0859 HOURS

WELFARE STATE DEATH GRIP MUST BE BROKEN!
As I set back and watch all of the ado going on about raising the debt ceiling I just take the whole thing with a grain of salt. In the grand scheme of things it really doesn't matter if they raise it or not because all that is doing is buying just a wee little more time.

Either way it is not going to stop the welfare state from killing off both the USA and global economies. As a supposition example, if miraculous all of the USA's debt and financial problems were solved today, we as a nation will still be doomed.

The reason is money and lack of jobs are direct and obvious, but the real things that hold every society together is not so obvious and have rotted away to the very core because of the welfare state. Number one, the base and foundation for all human survival are the nuclear and extended family system.

Nothing can exist and be strong without a survival need, and the welfare state has took away that need for the strong nuclear family and left this great nation with no means to survive when the going get rough, and believe me tough times is just over the horizon. And the other two critical survival means of good morals and adequate emergency backup bartering capacity are practical nonexistence.

I know no one want to hear it, but I repeat again and again that the only thing that is going to save the USA and western civilization is the complete elimination of the minimum wage as a start. Nothing else can break the death grip the welfare state have on this nation's economic throat; otherwise the welfare state is going to finish off the kill. SIRMANS LOG: 23 JULY 2011, 0005 HOURS

INFLATION'S BIGGEST MYTH AND MISCONCEPTION!
The biggest misconception about inflation is that the mass printing of money by government is the cause of inflation, wrong. Government can print all of the money it wants to and that alone will not ignite the cost of living consumer inflation.

So, OK, the government prints up all of this worthless money? But, in order to ignite inflation it has to get that money to enough people on an individual basis to corrupt the natural balance between the merchant and the consumer. Handing out free unearned money on an individual basis that and that alone is the cause of the cost of living consumer inflation.

That is why I keep screaming so loud that government should never give out free unearned money on an individual basis. Sure, as a last resort when the nuclear and extended family, the church, the community, and social organizations all fail then government must come to the rescue. And even then government should help the poor by establishing government run commissaries, housing, and clinics, and using scrip or tokens to prevent destroying the USA national economy which has happened.

Now, about 80 years after the "New deal" and mass false shallow liberal thinking it is just the opposite with close to 95 percent of the American people looking to government as the first resort for survival help, Lord, what a shame. But, oh, no, my great God given wisdom is totally ignored, I don't believe the egg heads will ever detour from the gimmick laden economical course of least resistance we are on today.
SIRMANS LOG: 16 APRIL 2011, 1631 HOURS.

HEALING QUOTE:
QUOTE: "I can wish all people goodwill

through God which strengthens me." One can leave off the through God which strengthens me or substitute in place of God ones own deity.

Just repeat the quote to yourself as many times as necessary or until the storm passes over. No one else has to know what you are repeating to yourself.

I promise you if you have trouble on your job, in your marriage, or whatever, your stress will vanish, it is not a cure all, but, a stress free healing process will began.

True joy and happiness comes from within. But, you can't find it from within. You find it by caring, helping, and serving others!

DIABETES HELPFUL HINTS

Every diabetic should read labels and keep count of the amount of carbohydrates consumed. Carbohydrates are really what determine ones blood sugar level. If carbohydrates can be kept down to around 50g per meal it will go a long ways in controlling ones blood sugar level.

Meats and fats without anything added like sauces and gravies don't contain carbohydrates. Most leafy vegetables and others like greens beans, broccoli, cauliflower, and sweet peas average around

15g per 1/2 cup. It is the big 5 that can be enjoyed but really need to be kept under control, they are bread, rice, potatoes, pasta, and artificial sweets.

My healthy eating priority formula: Eat, fresh and raw when possible, cooked fresh, cooked frozen, and lastly cooked canned. However, as a rule eating food properly cooked is always safer in my view. I'm not a trained medical professional in any way; I'm a self-made writer and hope my limited knowledge will be helpful to someone in some way.

USA AS GLOBAL ECONOMIC SLAVE!
Government as a super social and family provider means economic suicide when given enough time. It's simply impossible to make it work in economic terms. So far we have manage to get away with it since the "New deal" but the Jig is up, natures supreme law of "Natural selection" has finally chased us down and we are gonna pay dearly.

An economy has only two players a seller and a buyer and "supply and demand" is what they operate on. It doesn't matter how modern, complicated, or big an economy is that is still the process that makes any economy work over the long haul. A free market place that allow free competition is the only system know to man that has never failed to always produce an over abundance of everything.

With a minimum wage and mountains of red tape the USA is no longer even in the Ball Park in terms of a free market place economy. Government is not part of an economy but is a necessary parasite needed to safeguard and protect the whole society.

The people started off trading and bartering and evolved into using a currency to buy and sell. Generating a profit is the life blood that drives every successful economy.
Profit is what government takes in the form of taxes and is what allows government to exist.

Our government was designed to take only enough profit to safeguard and protect the nation, but the "New deal" opened up a small gate into a provider swamp. Now around eighty years later flood gates are wide open leading into a giant government provider swamp. Government is taking more and more profit in the form of higher and higher taxes and has become a full fledged super provider from cradle to grave.

With this going on it will be impossible not to suck any profit generating economy dry, we are done, cooked and ready to be served. This is why plead so hard for people to see the wisdom of completely eliminating the minimum wage, the free market place is the only thing that is going to feed us and keep us alive. Big government and red tape got a strangle hold on the USA economy and it can never be broken as long as a minimum wage is in place.

Ninety five percent of the USA population can't see pass the amount of money. Its nonsense to thank in terms of a thousand dollars when thirty years ago a dollar would buy more, it is the same with a minimum wage, it just make things unreal and distorts the whole economy, get rid of the minimum wage and it will save us from total doom.

Only as a last resort the government must help the poor but it should never give out free money on an individual basis that destroys the natural balance between the merchant and the consumer and drives inflation out of sight like we have today. The only way government can help the poor and not destroy the main economy is to provide government run kitchens, housing, and clinics and use tokens or script.

That way the economy will be kept in balance and the nation can then afford to repair the infrastructure and everything else like before the "New deal." Unless my advice or something like it is taken the country and whole infrastructure is going to unravel in the not too distance future.

The egg heads are not going to change, if the people don't take the bull by the horns and vote out these liberals soon we all are going to be at each others throat. I will repeat, if the minimum wage is not eliminated and the red tape slate not wiped clean the USA will end up as a slave to the global economy in my view.
SIRMANS LOG: MAY 31, 2011, 1637 HOURS

GUN TO HEAD CARD SWIPE!!!
The credit card swipe fee is a good example of free market thinking, which very few truly understand today. As a committed free market thinker I believe the government should just butt out of the whole credit card swipe fee matter, but I know it won't.

Good intentions are always subjective and not free market thinking. A banks survival depends on making a profit, but the retailers that is charged the swipe fee is not forced to pay the fee. So, what is the problem with that? There is no gun to the retailer's head making him use the service.

That is a balance between a buyer and a seller and it will always work itself out and seek a natural level if the government just butts out. The retailer can pass the cost on or just completely refuse to participate. The retailer can give cash discounts for paying cash or unlimited ways to deal with the situation.

But, in the end the banks can never charge more than the free market place can bear and stay in business. It is government control that distorts and destroys a natural balance between the buyer and the seller.
With government involvement what can happen is fewer and fewer bank will offer customer friendly innovated card services in the future.

I have no gripe either way. I consider myself just a free market place thinker and not a judge or jury either way. But, the trend and norm today is to do the right thing and be fair which in the end always creates inefficiency and excessive waste.
SIRMANS LOG: JUNE 8, 2011, 0851 HOURS

PEOPLE TAKE NOTES!
NEW ENTRY: 27 JUNE 2011, 1159 HOURS
Here I go self-aggrandizing again, but, if it get through to just one thick scull to me its worth it. Here I am a poor uneducated phobia ridden insecure neurotic South Georgia USA country boy writing on the world stage, only in America.

I don't know where my great wisdom comes from; it must be destiny or a gift from God. It's not normal, I don't know if its supernatural or what, all I know is it is real, and somebody better listen. There I said it, you can dismiss me as a nut case, right wing kook, nut, and loon or pick your choice of words, but you won't logically prove me wrong.

Enough said, now lets get down to brass tacks, I don't know or have never read any of the great economic thinkers, everything I say about economic is ninety nine percent my own creative thinking. Everything I know about learned economic thinking is derived from a pamphlet I read about thirty five years ago that said "All economies starts with bartering."

My great mind took that statement and can now dissect an economy with perspective that fits it into the over all grand design of human survival. I don't believe anyone can truly understand economics unless they have a basic understanding of how nature works.

The first law in understanding nature is to know that all survival is based on cycles otherwise there could be no existence. No matter what, real or imagined, if it didn't have a die and rebirth cycle one individual thing would crowd out the entire universe.

So, the thing about an economy and everything else in existence, no matter what system, it is designed by nature to collapse at some point. Sure, man with knowledge can manipulate and extend the collapse time for an economy, but the greater the extend time the greater the effect.

Before modern time the boom and bust cycle was around every seven years but the effect was small and the Nuclear and extended family system, the strong religious and moral code, and emergency backup bartering capacity with many small farmers and home gardeners just took over until the rebirth boom cycle kicked in again, and the following bust cycle was mostly a nuisance.

Nothing has really change the cycle is just a lot longer and it may take us back to the stone age if we don't rebuild a strong nuclear and extended family system. So, I hope you see, in terms of overall human survival there are thing far more important than just the economy, civilization survived on trade and bartering long before money and a currency was invented.

I keep preaching that if western civilization is to survive without going back to the Stone Age the nuclear and extended family system must be rebuilt. Nature's supreme law Of "Natural selection" uses a survival need to determine what exist or doesn't exist. If anything doesn't have a survival need it will slowly cease to exist.

The nuclear and extended family system will slowly cease to exist because the welfare state takes away its survival need. To sum it up, sure, the economy leg of the four legged survival stool is important, but far more important for human survival is the other three legs of the survival stool because every economy is going to collapse, it is only a matter of when.
NEW ENTRY ENDS

IDEOLOGY DISRESPECT IS REAL REASON FOR USA ECONOMIC FAILURE!
JUNE 12, 2011, 1435 HOURS, NEW ENTRY.
There are only two major things that are going to save the USA economy and western civilization, I don't care what the egg heads and learned economist tells you.
Those two things are a genuine free market place and a strong nuclear and extended family system, which today both are in shambles.

We have a provider welfare state and it is impossible for the USA government to continue carrying that financial burden any longer. And anybody dumb or economically ignorant enough to think that it can be continued doesn't deserve freedom. In some of my other articles I have drawn a blue print on how to accomplish the task of rebuilding our nuclear family system and fixing the economy which will be almost from scratch. NEW ENTRY END.

IDEOLOGY DISRESPECT IS REAL REASON FOR USA ECONOMIC FAILURE!

Ideology is not built on what I think, you think, or what anyone else thinks, it is based on what has been proven by trial and error for over 5000 years of civilization. We know that the Ideology of socialism has never been proven to work successful, yet, it just won't go away and people keep coming up with a new twist on the same failure system.

We also know that a genuine true "Free market place" ideology that allows free competition has never failed to over produce, yet, the powerful always runs away from it, I believe it is because of its harsh discipline, it hinders favoritism and who you know, if you don't produce you are gone! The thing that sets me apart in economic terms from the egg heads is our views on ideology.

The egg heads are schooled and believe that man can successful manage an economy with fact and figures alone, I don't believe that is possible except within the bound of ideology. We know without a doubt that the "Free market place" works, but why? I believe the main reason why it works is it allows nature's supreme law of "Natural selection" to weed out excuses, inefficiency, and waste.

In economic terms you can call that law the "Invisible hand" or whatever but that is the real master of every economy. Sure, for 80-100 years almost any system may work, then it's Katy bar the door, and that is where we are at today. The egg heads think they can save the USA economy with all kinds of schemes and government controls, but I'm here to tell you it ain't gonna happen.

The best thing the government can do is get the hell out of the way and let a genuine true free market place work its magic. Human survival can best be described as a four legged stool, and the "Free market place" ideology is only one leg of that stool. The first leg and most important one in my view is the nuclear and extended family ideology leg of that stool.

Ever since the dawn of history there has never been a society that survived long term without a strong nuclear and extended family system, which the welfare state has almost completely destroyed in the African American community. The second leg of the four legged survival stool is every society must have a strong religious and moral code in place to protect future generations; otherwise no one will give a damn about anything except themselves in the now.

The third leg of the stool is a society must have adequate back up bartering capacity through many small farmers and home gardeners in case the economy collapses. Like life itself everything must have a collapse or rebirth cycle after a period of time or moral decay and every other kind of inefficiency and waste will get too big and choke of survival.

The fourth and final leg of the four legged stool is an economy which only involved trade and bartering long before money was invented. The first currency was always something physical, and then paper money was always backed by something physical, now it is only backed by faith and the worth of the paper it is printed on. If inflation and taxes doesn't eat you alive with real estate at least you have something physical that won't go up in smoke.

Because of our welfare state the USA simply doesn't have enough people growing food and that means millions of people are going to starve when this global economy collapses, no one know when but everything must have a collapse or rebirth cycle to exist.

The reason why man can't run a successful economy with facts and figures alone is because there are simply too many variables

many of which are subjective, such as whose back is being scratched or who is under the desk and on and on.
SIRMANS LOG: JUNE 10, 2011, 1817 HOURS

LATE ENTRY: 28 JUNE 2011, 1200 HOURS
A PERFECT EXAMPLE OF WHY ONLY NATURE CAN DEAL WITH TOO POWERFUL ANTI-SURVIVAL FORCES IS THE RECENT NEW YORK LAW ALLOWING SAME SEX MARRIAGES.
There is something called a survival instinct that discipline and struggle instills in one which results in wisdom. Anyone with an ounce of wisdom by instinct alone will know that same sexes don't produce offspring and will ultimately lead to human extinction.

Yet, very few care or recognize that as a moral threat or for that matter even know what the hell a moral threat is. No problem, y'all. And the beat goes on. Whoa, what about Christian outrage? Oh, that, they are all out to lunch, y'all. And the beat goes on.

A moral threat is anything that threatens the unborn and future generations. A moral threat may not be as immediately as a physical threat but given time the result will come to the same conclusion, human extinction.

The main purpose of a religion in the first

place is to safeguard and protect morals; if I want a meeting place just to socialize I can do that in a dance hall.
LATE ENTRY ENDS.

WILL OBAMACARE SURVIVE?
UPDATE: 23 JANUARY 2011, 1243 HOURS.

What I see and understand so clearly on how an economy really work is simple, yet it shocks me why so few get it. Now almost everyone is focused on medical insurance, who got it, who can't get it, and on and on.

The Lib's rammed this Obamacare down our throats and believes that is the magic answer. I think all of that is missing the root problem with paying for medical care in America.

The root problem with medical care in America is "The lack of market forces due to the Federal government involvement." That involvement created the deadly side effect known as "Ultra-high-cost."

So, that makes "Mr. Ultra-high-cost" the real true villain in medical care. The government itself can't pay ultra-high-cost and 90 percent of the American people can't pay ultra-high-cost.

All any insurance company does is collect

enough money from a lot of healthy well people and bet not too many of them will become sick at any one time.

Insurance companies won't have the money if more than just a few of their customers become sick at a time, which means they can't afford "Mr. ultra-high-cost."

So, the shallow minded liberals decided they would solve the whole problem by forcing every able body adult to pay for medical insurance or go to jail, which I think is a dictator tactic, and un-American.

They figured that would produce enough healthy well people paying into the system to satisfy "Mr. ultra-high-cost," and in theory that should work. But, that can never work when not enough people have jobs. Then it all boils down to the bottom line.

Before any business can make one red cent of profit or pay one employee's salary it first must pay a yearly business license fee, permit fees, federal income taxes, state income taxes, local option taxes, social security tax, unemployment tax, medicare tax, state sales taxes, and taxes I can't even think of, plus satisfy all kinds of government red tape mandates.

Oh! I had forgotten to include having to make rent or mortgage payments too before the first penny of profit is made. I can't remember the statistics on the survival rate of all new startup businesses, but I think it is less than three percent still standing after five years.

On top of all of that everybody including the healthy young people is going to be hit with a new big whopping Obamacare health care tax.

Then and only then after paying all of that a business must try to find enough profit left to pay the employees, restock, take care of utilities, do maintenance and then live off what is left, it is no wonder why there are no jobs. Plus, some utility companies piles on by charging a business almost twice the rate that they do the public.

I believe when the Obamacare impact fully hits the jobless rate is going to sky rocket even higher than it is now, and then you add all of the welfare state dead beats, that is a lot of people not paying into the system.

If Obamacare survives I just don't think there are going to be enough people paying into the system even if they do start giving the old folks pain pills and sending them on their way.

In fact at this stage I know beyond a shadow of doubt that eliminating the "Minimum wage" and kicking the welfare state out of its social and family provider role is the only thing that's going to save the USA.

The family provider role must be restored back to the head of household where it belongs and where it always was until the "New deal" came along. That must be done or this great nation perishes.

Everyone keep griping about not making a living wage, but I will guarantee you that is a losing battle because the bigger the government the farther the cost of living out distances a living wage, there is no getting around that fact.

The only way to solve that is to get the government to stop giving out free money on an individual basis. If that is done the cost of living will have to come down to where poor people can pay their own medical bills and other cost, simply because the government will no longer be subsidizing and driving up prices.

Without the government subsidizing high prices by giving out free money on an individual basis very few merchant can charge more than the poor can pay and stay in business.

Sure, the government should help the poor and not let anyone starve, but do that by setting up temporary commissaries, kitchens, shelters, clinics, or whatever.

But, don't destroy the county's free market place, its culture, and everything else by giving out free money on an individual basis, that is what ignited the killing inflation that is eating us alive today.

Right now no one wants to hear my no "Minimum wage" solution, but they will, just wait, its coming, mass starving is right around the corner, you'll see.

Come on folks! Y'all got eyes and a brain! What goes here? Sometimes I wonder if the liberals really are this economically ignorant or just want go ahead and push this great nation on over the cliff. They are still speeding up government spending instead trying to cut back.

I know it's unthinkable, but what if they are trying to force martial law for a once and for all absolute government take over, government already owns 90 percent of the real estate market and big chunks of the manufacturing industry. Maybe I'm crazy to think out loud like this. Lord have mercy on my soul.

Using tunnel vision and looking at survival one dimensional through the economy prism only is the deadly mistake most egg heads and ninety five percent of the population are making.

All, even a real physical currency does is make trade and bartering a zillion times more convenient. Civilization has never survived only on faith and I don't believe it can today, and paper money is just that.

Civilization can and did survive on trade and bartering long before money was invented, but no society or nation is going to survive very long without all four legs of the survival stool holding strong, otherwise the nation will soon fall from within.

You can call it culture or whatever, but I see the first leg of the four legged survival stool as a strong nuclear and extended family system. The second leg I see as a strong moral and religious code in place.

The third leg I see as adequate bartering capacity backup in case the economy fails. That requires many small farmers and home gardeners, and with no citizen expecting the government to guarantee their survival.

And the fourth and last leg I see as the economy with a stable currency. Now, if anyone thinks we in the USA have a stable currency, good for you, I'm not so sure.

Being able to see all four legs of what I

believe is the survival stool in perspective I think raises me above the tunnel vision and one dimensional thinking that so many so called smart people fall prey to.

Again, I write what I think, I don't try to tell anybody what to think, and I might be a snake oil salesman myself for all you know. Do your own thinking and check more than one source.

If you don't see any validity in what I write just continue writing me off as a nut case and believe what the liberals tell you. Thank you for taking the time to read this article, and may God bless you. With love always, yours truly, bye.
SIRMANS LOG: 20 JANUARY 2011, 1736 HOURS.

THE RANTING OF A LUNATIC, YOU DECIDE? Like I've said before, I understand how an economy truly works as well as anyone I don't care how many degrees they have. And I'm here to tell you I believe all the recent spending cuts is going to do is speed up the demise and day of reckoning of our welfare state.

I don't want to be right on this, almost no one believes me anyway, so, let everyone just continue on their merry way. Sure, before the "New deal" and even on up to the late seventies cutting government spending would have reduced the size of government.

But, not any more there are far too many social programs waiting to kick in and over compensate for every spending cut advantage thereby vastly growing big government even more with an ever increasing dole population.

Plus, today this welfare state has grown into this super beast that has all but destroyed our nuclear and extended family system and all of the rest of the pre "New deal" survival infrastructure.

It is not too late to save individual freedom and the last bastion of true freedom in the world today, but the options are down to survival or getting big government out of its super provider role.

Until big government is de-clawed out of its all power super provider role no political party or anything else is going to keep it from spending this nation into total doomsday oblivion.

I try not to promote self in my writing but I do want to stress a point, I have the depth, the wisdom, the perspective, and the awareness that very few have, and I believe beyond a shadow of a doubt that these spending cut are going to put this great nation in a do or die situation.

Caution, get ready for mass unemployment almost beyond the imagination. Caution; get ready for the dole population to increase like never before because the liberals, the head of household women, and the countless special interest groups are going to start screaming bloody murder about these spending cuts affect on social programs.

And I will be agreeing with them, because in a welfare state it is unfair to cold turkey throw people to the wild without providing a life line. The nuclear family system has been ripped to threads by the welfare state and that have left masses upon masses of people that have never been conditioned to survive without the government dole.

Abandoning these people is like setting a tame animal loose into the wild, it would have little chance of survival. The politicians will not be able to resist it; a tax raise will be imposed on the fewer and fewer surviving businesses thereby driving the final nail in the coffin.

I, Freddie L. Sirmans, Sr. have thrown out a survival life line and it is being completely ignored, my view is a drowning man shouldn't be choosey. No one will take me serious; I know the egg heads will never listen to my great wisdom because I don't have a Yale degree or for that matter even any college degree.

However, I must do my duty and pass it on regardless. Here is my survival solution, it is no cure all, and it is only a mean to prevent a total meltdown with millions upon millions starving to death in the USA.

No one will win but we will survive. The first order of business is the death grip the welfare state has on our nation's economic throat must be broken before there is any chance of this nation surviving with freedom intact.

If the nation doesn't have the will or guts to take this drastic step then you might as well stop reading, my solution is then out of the question. I will lay out three steps to prevent the total meltdown of the USA economy.

(1.) To break the welfare state death grip the first thing that must be done is the "Minimum wage" must be completely eliminated because in free market place economics terms that is like a vehicle with no reverse or a water heater with no pop off valve.

(2.) In the USA the nuclear family system is almost totally destroyed from lack of need because of the welfare state, that means the government must never abandon these people without giving them a life line until the nuclear family system is restored.

Sure, these people must be helped but government must never give anyone free money on an individual basis, because that is what destroys the balance between the merchant and the consumer. That is what causes inflation and is the cause of the out of control inflation we have today.

(3.) Under current conditions the government must provide help to the poor and disadvantage but never by giving out unearned money on an individual basis. Government must provide temporary government commissaries, housing, and clinics to keep people alive until the nuclear and extended family system is rebuilt in this nation.

Also, to keep government spending from contaminating the free market place some type of script or tokens must be use for those qualifying for government help. A true free market place economy has never failed in the history of civilization because nature's law of "Natural selection" weeds out inefficiency. It is only through government interference instead of just collecting the taxes that kills every economy.

The nuclear and extended family system is how people survived for over 5000 years before the "New deal" came along and

created this super welfare state beast, and there is not enough money in the whole wide world to keep this beast fed.
SIRMANS LOG: 9 APRIL 2011, 2029 HOURS.

Economic wise, all of the spending cuts and taxes remaining the same are going to do is take a smaller pie out of the oven.

The only thing that is going to stop this runaway economy is booting the welfare state out of the all powerful social and family provider role, by eliminating the minimum wage as a first step. After the government first establish community wise only emergency kitchens, shelters, and clinics

A CURRENT EVENT ISSUE:
I saw on TV where two small minority talk radio hosts are going all out to try to destroy the biggest talk radio show host. They say it is in the name of protecting the public from race baiting. I think what they fail to understand is what free speech is truly all about.

Free speech is not just about what we agree with and want to hear, it is more about protecting that speech we disagree with and don't want to hear. Hell, I feel anyone that genuine love and accept their own true self-identity will not feel threaten by every so called race baiting insensitive comment, because what is good for the goose is good for the gander.

I am already secure on who I am and stuff like that to me is like water off a ducks back. The key is to love and accept all people even if it is not returned, especially those of your own race who look like you.

No one is perfect and everyone has flaws, even if they don't show. Many, many people will totally disagree with everything I just said; still I have a right to say it under the five freedoms listed in the 1st amendment to the constitution of the United States of America.
SIRMANS LOG: ON THIS 69th PEARL HARBOR ANNIVERSARY DECEMBER 7, 1941, I WRITE THIS TODAY 1201 HOURS.
23 NOVEMBER 2010 1527 HOURS:

New update on air line search techniques. I think the air lines, the workers, and all involved are trying their level best to make the best of a bad situation and keep the flying public safe. Then on the other hand you have this negative constant drumbeat by much of talk radio and other arm chair quarter backs second guessing the best safety possible for the American flying public.

What this could end up doing is forcing the

management into lesser security. Then guess what? Who do you think may end up taking much of the blame and heat if a plane ends up being blown out of the sky? Need I say more?

A CURRENT EVENT ISSUE: 22 NOVEMBER 2010, 2205 HOURS:
New comment on air line search technique. I think a few people are trying to keep a bandwagon going. Being patted down is not new, you go back over 40 to 50 year before modern metal detecting devices and it was not uncommon at all for some night clubs to do pat downs.

Its been over 50 years when I was a young man I along with everyone else was patted down before enter a night club and no one raised any hell about it. No court is going to touch this with a ten foot pole, because then they would be responsible for what ever happens.

The people raising so much hell don't have to answer for anything if a plane is blown up.

THE AIRLINES SEARCH TECHNIQUE!
Let me get this out of the way first, having the pilots go through the same search technique is nonsense in my view. However, folks if not the strict search technique, what

is your solution?

Right now the same folks pissing and moaning the loudest will be the same ones complaining the loudest if their loved ones are on a plane that blows up. Come on folks, no one has a gun to anyone's head telling them that they gotta fly.

Take your voyage by ship or other means if it's that bothersome. What are you going to tell your urologist if you have a medical problem, it is the same with the intent not to be sexual in any way? At the rate of technology advancement today a better remedy should come about very soon.

But, until that happens, I say fly safe and live because it is not about any one individual. I seen a lady on TV get all angry and rebellious, but, she could never come up with a real or better solution, which is the case with most of the get on the bandwagon complainers.

The vast majority of the people doing that type of work dislike the technique as much as you, but these people have family to feed. And their management has a responsibility to keep everyone alive. Talk is cheap.

F L SIRMANS, SR. PLEAS FOR DIVINE HELP! The thing about me that make my great thinking so awesome is it is not limited in any way; it has no borders or boundaries.

I have never been to economic school or taken any such classes! I don't know what is not supposed to work! Almost all of my thinking is original; it is raw and creative from the core! Plus, my thinking takes in vastly more than the economic one leg of the whole survival stool.

I'm more of a deep thinking philosopher that sees the whole survival stool and how the economy fits into the grand design. There are infinite variables in an economy many are subjective which makes it impossible to be manage by man even with a super computer.

What actually runs every economy no matter the type of government is nature's supreme law of "Natural selection." Sure, almost any liberal bleeding heart do good economic system may work for 80-100 years, but, then the consequences of ignoring nature's supreme law of "Natural selection" catches up.

And then someone is gonna pay in blood, sweat, or tears. The nuclear and extended family system is the foundation of human survival. And is protected under nature's supreme law of "Natural selection." So, when the welfare state for all practical purpose destroyed our nuclear and extended family system the consequences is going to make us pay dearly, hopefully we will survive as a nation.

I'm paraphrasing when I say someone complained that democracy was a terrible form of government but is still the best government known to man. That is why I often wonder why is it so hard for nations to use an economic ideology that has never failed and have proven to always work time and time again.

It will always produce an over abundance of everything. That ideology is: "Allow free competition and let the free market place work." I think the real reason is governments just love power and the ability to control too much. Another cold hard fact on that matter is:

It is impossible to "Have free competition and a free market place" with government finger all in the pie. The more government gets involve the less of a free market place you will have. When government sets a minimum wage which is like a vehicle with no reverse and enacts every kind or regulation and mandate one can imagine that means our USA economy

doesn't even come close to being a free market place. That being the case, no one has to tell me that a total collapse is possible.

In the distance past a collapsing economy was something almost normal. It was just a rebirth or renewal. The strong nuclear and extended family system along with plenty bartering capacity would keep order until enough new growth kicked in.

We no longer have that safety valve anymore, western welfare states has just about destroyed that entire infrastructure. We no longer have a strong reliable nuclear and extended family structure anymore everybody is depending on our welfare state daddy.

Much of our moral and religious code has been reduced to what comes out of Hollywood. And we no longer have enough backup emergency bartering capacity in small farmers and home gardeners like what got us through the great depression.

This welfare state super beast has left this great nation with almost nothing in term of bare boned survival in time of crisis. We as a nation could face almost total chaos. GOD, I ASK IN YOUR NAME, SAVE OUR GREAT NATION! SIRMANS LOG: 9 NOVEMBER 2010, 1830 HOURS

MY QUICK BRIEF ANALYSIS OF LIBERALISM! I'm going to make a short brief analysis of liberalism and not make this a long drawn out detailed analysis. The first thing is there is nothing innate about being a liberal.

Liberalism is basically a lack of survival awareness. To put it more bluntly liberals tend to be shallow with a weak survival instinct. I'm not saying that to be mean and put down liberals in a negative way.

Life is about balance, no one thing in a person's life make one person better or lesser than another. I wouldn't want to live in a world without liberals because it would be too hard, cruel, and without the tender side of life.

Besides, many a liberal has been converted overnight to a conservative, especially if a mugger slammed them upside the head and robber them. I understand why liberals don't understand me and see me as some kind of kook or nut case.

The main reason is they can't see what I see. They don't have the depth and awareness that I have. I can see everything a liberal can see plus much, much more than a liberal will ever see simply because they have never fought a life time of mental battles like I have.

It is like buying a new car. All of a sudden you see cars of your make and model all over the place. Nothing has changed they were out there all of the while it's just that you were not aware of them. It is the same with knowing what it takes to survive.

If you have never had real test struggles on what it takes to survive you won't know what threats there are out there. That is why almost nothing of any real and lasting value can be accomplished without struggle and hardship.

I'm not special of have any kind of monopoly on wisdom. There are many people out there that have had it a lot worse than I have. And never forget that there is an exception to everything in nature. Hardship and struggle affects people in two ways.

It will make most people more humble and caring and overall a better human being. And a few it will make more and more bitter. I thank God it has made me a very humble and caring human being with super natural wisdom.

To fail to prepare a child how to be independent and stand on his own as a productive citizen eighteen years later is not real love and caring. That is irresponsible parenting!
SIRMANS LOG: 8 NOVEMBER 2010, 0203 HOURS

SPENDING CUTS WON'T STOP THE DOOM OF WESTERN CIVILIZATION!

7 NOVEMBER 2010, LAST UPDATE: 0839 HOURS
CURRENT EVENT:
I think both President Bush's 41 and 43 did a great job in protecting and safeguarding the Supreme Court. And I for one will forever sing their praise. But, I believe they both were good, proud and decent Rockefeller type republicans, also.

FOOLED BY THE GIFT OF GAB AND SLIGHT OF HAND!

The liberals are experts at the gift of gab and blame shifting but I will never be fooled because I watch more of what one does than a lot of false promises and empty rhetoric.

Liberals know they can never admit their true goals and intentions and get elected. The liberals are saying almost all of the right things, but, look at their action record for the last couple of years.

Their action record has been to grow big government like never before, not take any responsibility for their own actions, keep shifting all blame to someone else, government take over of most of the private auto industry, government take over of 90 percent of the private real estate market, screwing up the private insurance industry by almost doubling the price if you can still get it, and then to try to take over as much of the private sector as they can, which I believe is to make the USA a fully socialist country.

Their record is not hidden; it is right there for all to see what is really taking place in broad daylight. That is all the proof of liberal's intentions anyone need. God save this last bastion of true freedom in the world today.

I am under no illusion, I know the stuff I write is rejected by almost everyone, and still, I must keep sounding the alarm even if no one takes heed.

I can assure you as long as government is a mass family provider nothing or no one is going to stop the growth of government. Sure, the tea party and conservatives will slow down the growth of government but they will find it impossible to stop all growth.

The reason is 95 percent of the American people don't see anything wrong with government in a provider role. There is no painless way to fix our economy and whoever actually makes painful drastic cuts are going to be voted out of office.

That is the pickle this nation is in. There has never been a nation that has changed course knowing it was headed toward disaster in the history of mankind. That is because those in power will never voluntarily release their death grip even if the nation goes down in flames.

The founding fathers put most of the real power in the hands of the people and the states, but, the people and the states gave up their real power. The states gave up their real power by giving up the right to appoint two senate representatives every six years.

And the American people give up their real power by allowing the federal government to seize and keep the family provider role for itself. Whoever carries out the family provider role is the boss and rules the country.

It hasn't finished consolidating it power yet, but the federal government already carries out a big enough percentage of the family provider role to stop all serious attempts at reducing its size. Very few government dependents are going to vote against the hand that feeds them.

This whole nation including the economy and everything else is now built around supporting one giant super welfare state beast. There is not enough money in the entire world to keep this beast fed.

But, if this beast is not fed our whole way of life will collapse into a giant dust heap, that is the pickle we are in. As I keep repeating with my great supernatural wisdom, the only controllable way to save this great nation with freedom still intact is to eliminate the minimum wage entirely, period.

We no longer have much of a choice; our whole economic system could collapse any day now. The first rule in economics is: you can't get blood out of a turnip.

That means no business can charge more than the poor people can afford to pay and stay in business because there is almost never enough rich and middle income people to keep a business profitable.

That is if government just stop subsidizing prices with welfare and food stamps and gets the hell out of the way. Then the price of everything and the ability to pay will seek a balance down where most of the poor can pay for their own food and medical cost out of pocket.

And those that can't pay should then have government run community shelters, kitchens, and clinics to turn to. The really sad thing is this nation's whole survival is at stake, and most people don't even have a clue.

CURRENT EVENT:
THE FIRING OF JUAN WILLIAMS!
I believe Juan Williams is a genuine liberal. I have seen him over the years on many programs. And I disagree with almost everything he says, yet I like Juan Williams.

In my view Juan Williams is no phony yes man that always goes along to get along. I think he is loved and respected by so many because it shines through that he is a truly honest and decent man.

Again, I almost totally disagree with him on everything, but, it is in my nature to respect decency and honesty no matter who has it. I think Juan Williams has that and no one can take that asset away.

I seldom comment on current events, but on this matter I felt a need to weigh in.

ABOUT SPENDING CUTS!
Spending cuts won't save welfare state economies because that is not striking at the heart of the matter. The root of the problem is government cannot take on the nuclear family provider role on a large scale without destroying the culture and everything in it.

All spending cuts are going to do is pit one

group against another and speed up the
process to doom. Right now all four legs of
the survival stool are beginning to collapse.
The whole system is out of balance due to
violations of nature's supreme law of "natural
selection."

It is those consequences that are now
catching up with us. There are no free rides
in nature someone always pays one way or
another. The violations started with the "New
deal" when government seized the nuclear
and family provider role for itself but failed to
maintain family discipline.

The liberals done this to keep power by
handing out goodies with tax payers money
and is still trying to keep it up to this day.
That was the poison pill that is about to kill
our economy around 80 years later. There is
no saving western civilization until
government is kicked out of the nuclear and
extended family provider role, period.

Money or the lack of money today is not
everything but seem to be the only thing that
matters. But, the truth is civilization survived
with trade and bartering long before money
was invented.

The four legs of the survival stool are: (1.)
The nuclear and extended family system, (2.)
a strong religious and moral code, (3.)
adequate emergency bartering capacity with

many small farmers and home gardeners, and (4.) the economy and money with a physical backed currency.

Now, everyone is zeroing in on cutting spending, especially social spending. I urge caution, when the government has irresponsible created masses upon masses of dependents with no knowledge of how to survive solely on their own it cannot just walk away.

These people need to be conditioned to be responsible and think for themselves. Government must provide on a wide scale community wise emergency shelters, kitchens, and clinic. There is no doubt in my mind if the government get out of the way the free enterprise system with entrepreneurs will save the USA with its freedom intact.

But, one way or another government must give up its nuclear and extended family provider role or all is lost. No matter what the egg heads tell you, I guarantee you this ship is going down unless the minimum wage is gotten rid of entirely, I can't see any other way.

After first establishing community wise emergency shelters, kitchens, and clinics, then by eliminating the minimum wage it will allow a slow manageable means of avoiding a total collapse of the whole system. A total collapse could mean 100 million or more starving to death.

With all of my great wisdom on the line that is my analysis of the situation we as a nation are in. To not pass this on in my view would be a dialect of duty on my part. No one has to believe me or even take me serious.

If you think I'm a kook or my analysis is totally crap I assure you not everyone thinks as you do. What is your solution? If you have a better one, please share it, I have a comment section on my website.

The sun shall not smite thee by day nor the moon by night.
SIRMANS LOG: 21 OCTOBER 2010, 1055 HOURS

HOW TO DEFUSE OUR WELFARE STATE DESTRUCTION TIME BOMB!

15 OCTOBER 2010: LAST UPDATE, 0819 HOURS
Having the USA government fulfilling the role of the "Great white father" super colossal social and family provider is like having the fox guarding the hen house.

There is no way our all power welfare state is going to continue tolerating individual freedom in the USA because it already has the power to tax at will and take what it wants to continue ruling over us like we are peons.

The Supreme Court and no law are going to stop it unless the minimum wage is completely eliminated, period. Then the people can take back the family provider role for themselves and the government will be dependent on the will of the people like the founding fathers designed it.

CURRENT EVENT:
A SUPER COLOSSAL MISTAKE IN MY VIEW!
I think one of the dumbest and naive political moves I've seen lately is the denying being a witch political Ad. All that did was focus on the negative and give legs to something no one would have given a damn about except the shallow liberal news media.

Instead of her relentlessly pounding on no jobs and too high taxes which is a sure winner she allowed herself to be sucked into the mire of a juicy personal issue by trying to disprove a negative, which is almost impossible. Still, it's better late than never to right the ship.

My unsolicited advice is get out front, let the voters decide, don't be shy, ask them which political party will most likely control wasteful spending and help the private sector provide real lasting jobs, not big government temporary make work jobs.

The obvious political party that will do all of that is a no brainier, let the voter decides. Whoever wins, hopeful the people will have heard both sides and not one side drowned out by a lot of emotional nonsense?

STAY ON MESSAGE, LOWER UNEMPLOYMENT AND LOWER TAXES AND DON'T GET SIDE TRACKED!
Most candidates get side tracked because of the mass news media.

The media will bite on just about anything and run like hell with it if there is even a hint of smut or dirt involved. But, obsessing on juicy and personal stuff leaves voters without a sensible option and in almost all cases works against a conservative.

The liberals will go to the extreme in tossing the media some bait to help lure a conservative away from lower taxes and more jobs. I believe the Brown case is an example of trying to keep the focus away from high unemployment and too high taxes.

A word to the wise, don't let the personal stuff throw you off message. The majority Productive citizen cares far more about more

jobs and less taxes than who did who.
HELLO?

Keep the drum beat going louder and louder
for more jobs and less taxes no matter how
loud the personal distractions is blasted about
you, then you can't lose with the stuff you
use.

HOW TO DEFUSE OUR WELFARE STATE
DESTRUCTION TIME BOMB!
Okay, let's get real and face the rock hard
cold steel facts. Starting with the "New deal"
the liberals from both major political parties
has created our big government monster size
social and family provider beast.

It has created countless government
dependents with many depended on
government for their only survival. What
surprises and scares the hell out of me is
around 95 percent of the American people
don't see anything wrong with government
being a super family provider and think that
is normal.

Nothing could be farther from normal; it's
insane for government to be a family provider
in a free country. No free country will remain
free with government in the all powerful role
of super family provider.

Going back over 5000 years until the "New

deal" came along the nuclear and extended family system always maintained with discipline the family provider role, then liberals in the name of government seized it for themselves solely to dish out goodies to keep power.

But, government refused to set standards, and then family discipline went out the window especially in the African American community. And even to this day no one is instilling self-restraint in most black males and they are filling up the prisons at an ever increasing rate.

I can't make you believe me but I'm still going to tell you the gospel truth anyway, there is no way in hell the USA is ever going to be saved from doom without rebuilding the nuclear family system as part of any solution. Now, chew on that!

Whoever is the family provider is the boss and has almost unlimited power over its dependents and in this case the voters. Whoever is your provider is your boss like it or not no matter how you spin it.

The only power we the people have left in America is our vote and that is practically useless in a real showdown because very few government dependents are going to bite the hand that feeds them.

Right now, you hear the Tea party talk and the talk about voting one team out and putting in a new slower team, drip, drip, dripping still ever so slowly toward full socialism. What we need is a halt and then a retreat no matter how slowly away from socialism.

But, until I actually see a retreat I believe it is still all talk because practically all of the real power is still in the hands of our all powerful sugar daddy welfare state provider. Really, do you people actually believe a new team in place is going to put a dent in social spending?

It has never been done in the past and I bet my bottom dollar it ain't gonna happen this time if we get a new team running the show. Sure, there will be a lot of talk and promises but nothing will have any real teeth in my view.

Around the world you see labor unions and others rioting in the street when even the smallest cut or changes are planned. Well, the same thing is going to happen in America when real change is seriously proposed. And for now I just don't think the voters are quite ready to do what must be done for this nation to survive.

There simply is no painless way out of the burdens and responsibilities the liberals have taken on for this nation to have to bear. I know the future may look hopeless but all is not lost. But, it's going to require some great wisdom I, Freddie L. Sirmans, Sr. can provide.

Whatever is done to save this great nation from total destruction must utilize the "Natural selection" process. Any piece meal cuts here and there are going to pit one group against the other to no end.

Forget about who may lose this or that the existence and survival of the nation itself is at stake. There is no avoiding deflation, plus deflation itself is not a bad thing, avoiding deflation is what got us in this dire mess in the first place.

The thing about deflation is it is harmless and healthy if brought about in a "Natural selection" process. On the other hand if it is managed solely by man it could mean everyone going for each others throat and total chaos.

Okay, first things first, before action is taken the goal should be to return the family provider role back to where it belongs with the nuclear and extended family system. If that is not the goal there is nothing I can do to help save this great nation.

If the goal is to save this great nation by

returning the provider role back where it belongs, here is my propose plan of action: Government should prepare by first setting up all around the country community wise only emergency shelters, kitchens, and clinics.

Once that is done, completely eliminate the minimum wage entirely, period. That will through the "Natural selection" process slowly start deflating the entire economy in a manageable way, however, there will be survival growing pains, but they will be bearable, the economy and country will survive with freedom still intact.

There will be many, many, more jobs and the whole system will start correcting itself. The whole process depends on the government returning the provider role back to a quickly rebuilding nuclear and extended family system and letting the private sector rebuild the free market place.

Government should focus on internal and external defense, community wise shelters, kitchens, and clinics, and collecting a lot less in taxes needed. Deflation will bring about a balance where all prices will start coming down to where the average working man and woman can live and pay their own medical cost out of pocket. It is not the amount of money that counts it's the buying power of money that truly matters.

This is my solution to help save this great country from collapsing into total chaos. If anyone else has a better solution step forward, then dismiss my plan of action. A word of advice, keep listening to the eggs heads that keep spouting the big government line and we all are going to be up S... creek without a paddle.

He that keepeth thee will not slumber. SIRMANS LOG: 29 SEPTEMBER 2010, 2049 HOURS.

The scariest thing in the world for a liberal is to get caught in a position where there is no one else to blame and he has take responsibility. To try to get a liberal to avoid shifting blame is like shoving a cross in the face of a vampire.

I really don't like to dwell too much on me when I write but there is a time for everything and I will be brief concerning me.

I know I don't have any real power to change anything or convince anyone else to make changes, however, no matter how small, I do believe I am offering enlightenment which can be a life line for this nations survival.

There is no doubt in my mind that I'm right on the vast majority of my analyses. I feel sooner or later more people will realize the validity of my great wisdom to aid in the survival of this great nation.

If I'm wrong I will continue to be almost completely ignored as a kook. But, if I'm truly right as I say I am all of the king's horses and all of the kings men are not going to be able to keep my talent and abilities from seeking their own level of greatness.

If God willing and the creek don't rise I will stay the course because persistent and determination alone are omnipotent. "My help cometh from God, he will not suffer thy foot to be moved."

No American business man wants to leave his own country and take away American jobs. But, first a business must survive both its competition and the ability to make a profit or it cease to exist.

What is really driving Americans jobs out of the country is the appetite demand of our welfare state to fund its super social and family provider role. The truth is the social and family provider role belongs to first the Nuclear and extended family system, the church, and community organizations, period.

As a last resort government should help out but only on a temporary basis. That has been the foundation for civilizations survival for over 5000 years until the "New deal" came along. I'm telling you economics is just one leg of the survival stool and it's not the most important one either.

If a nation doesn't have a dependable nuclear and extended family system in place along with a good moral and religious code no amount of money is going to save it from doom.

Yet, I hear the liberals blaming everybody and his brother for America's financial problems when they are the ones to blame for creating this super welfare state beast that want to provide cradle to grave care for everyone with tax payers money.

Hell, I would be for big government taking care of me and everybody, too, but I have sense enough to know it's impossible and it will destroy the country. Get a grip America before the liberals leave us all to perish.

Have you ever seen a chicken run around with its head cut off, I have and it's not a pretty sight?

I was born in 1942 and we lived on a farm. Many times I have seen my mother kill a chicken for dinner. There was sort of a chopping block in a back yard that you couldn't find a blade of grass anywhere.

My mother would fire up a huge pot of boiling water then go out to the hen yard and grab a pullet. She would take the pullet by both legs and hold its neck over that block, and then she would take a large machete like butcher knife and whack the head off with one swing.

She would then quickly sling the chicken out into the yard; the chicken would land on its feet and run headless like crazy in all directions for several seconds. The hot boiling water would permit the feathers to be easily pulled off.

Today most people don't realize it but anytime we eat meat someone had to perform a violent act necessary for our survival. That is what all of this activity involving the economy reminds me of. Almost everyone is running every which a way trying to come up with a solution.

I can guarantee you what the problem is in four words and it is what's destroying both the USA culture and economy, but reason and sanity has flown the coop; reality has yet to set in. And until these four words I'm talking about are dealt with nothing is going to work.

Way back before the nuclear weapon age of mutual destruction the authoritarian non-free market place governments survived by exploiting smaller and weaker states. Non-free market place states have never been able to feed its entire population except through slavery of some other type of exploitation.

Today no country can survive without a free market place unless it has natural resources to sell or receive outside help. "Government as a provider" is the four words I'm talking about and is the arch-villain that have all but destroyed our culture and economy.

Once government seized the provider role for itself and got drunk on the godlike power as a super provider, it don't ever plan on going back to just protecting and defending the country and doing only the things the people can't do for themselves.

As long as government is still in its super provider role we the people might as well kiss this great land of the free goodbye because nothing less than kicking government out of that role is going to save the USA from doom.

When government is in the role of super provider it has practically all of the real power and it is going to use that power to consolidate and protect that power, the country, manufacturing, jobs and everything else can go straight to hell as long as its provider role is protected.

You mark my words nothing less than kicking the government out of its super provider role is going to amount to a hill of beans.

Sure, government has a responsibility to help keep people alive by providing community wise things like community shelters, community kitchens, and community clinics, but anything more destroys the "Natural selection" need for the nuclear and extended family system. And that is the worst thing you can do to any society, because when the nuclear and extended family system goes culture decline soon follows, then the economy stalls and finally total doom.

When the nuclear and extended family can't help an individual then to the rescue should be the church and community organizations, and if all of that fails only then should the government help with community wise facilities.

There must be a survival need for the nuclear and extended family system or it will cease to exist. A welfare state destroys that need. Kicking the government out of it provider role is all it will take for the USA to survive and regain its greatness because nothing else is going to save us from total doom.

I know my God given great wisdom will be totally ignored but still I've did my duty. In life there are no free rides, sooner or later the day to pay the piper can't be put off any longer and must be paid in blood, sweat, or tears.

The energy and force that is driving this whole world wide decline of western civilization is the mostly big government liberals that are dead set on making more and more people government dependent.

Everything spins off of that driving force, you name it, high taxes, jobs going over seas, illegal immigrants, and every other ill of today is a direct result of liberals determine to finance their social and family provider role.

It is an impossible task because as more and more dependents are made you have fewer and fewer people paying into the system. Still, the liberals keep fooling enough voters with big promises and smooth talk to stay in power, what a sad situation.

I'm fixing to say something about me that is probably my wild imagination gone astray, but still it just may be an ounce of truth in it. Here goes, it is mind boggling how a shy neurotic insecure poor South Georgia USA country boy with only a high school formal education can raise up out of the ashes like a phoenix and influence world wide economic thinking.

That is truly a miracle that only destiny can bring about, if you doubt me just read some of my books found on any Internet search engine, Alias Freddie L Sirmans, Sr.

My miracle could never have happen before the Internet age. I agree my books may not always be top notch professionally written because everything is done solely by me. The formatting and grammar may not always meet the highest standard. But, none of that stops my supernatural great wisdom from shinning through.

When it comes to the bare bone survival of this nation many of my answers and solutions are unsurpassed. I believe what is at stake here is the survival of western civilization and capitalization itself.

I also believe my deep, deep wisdom bores through all of the smoke, fog and others distractions and strikes at the heart of the arch-villain (Government as a provider) that is about to take down the USA and western civilization.

Unless this villain is shot with a silver bullet or an iron stake driven through the heart the American people will never be able to regain enough power to stop this welfare state beast from selling this country's sovereignty to the U.N. or some new world body.

Sure, I'm going to be called a kook, nut case, and a host of other mentally disturbed names but still none of that will proves me wrong. Only History can prove me wrong and the wait won't be very much longer because I believe this whole global economy is on the brink of collapsing.

When you read my writing it is raw, crude, extreme, and undiluted by any editor or anyone just like when you drink your liquor straight with no chaser, only the rough and tough can take it.

I will lift up mine eyes unto the hills from whence cometh my help.
SIRMANS LOG: 6 SEPTEMBER 2010, 1721 HOURS.

FREDDIE L. SIRMANS, SR'S LOG: 23 AUGUST 2009, 2051 HOURS.
World wide the welfare state system is on the brink of destroying western civilization. It destroys a nation's culture, its morals, its family values, and any capacity to barter. But, nothing has been more devastated by the welfare state than the African American community in the USA.

The African American people in America have come a long ways. The African American people survived slavery, racism, and unbelievable odds to now have a biracial black man in the white house. A great deal of the credit must go to all Americans because only in America could this happen.

America is still the greatest and all Americans have so much to be proud of. I write what I think and feel and pull very few punches. I'm old enough and remember when I went to an all black high school and violence on campus was something almost unheard of.

I remember as a teenager when there were teen clubs and soda shops where teens could dance and hang out all over town. Now, there are none because there is too much drug use and violence. I remember when teens had almost complete respect for authority.

Now, a five year old will cuss you out. So, what changed? What happen? What went wrong? I'll tell you, the "New Deal and the welfare state" seized the family provider role for itself, that's what went wrong. It seized the provider role and refused to enforce responsibility and accountability in raising the young that came with it.

Once the black man was kicked out of the house there was no one to instill "Self-restraint" in young black males. Those two words "Self-restraint" and the lack of it is why there is so much violence in the African American community. And the welfare state is what destroyed the black nuclear family and community.

All of the young gang banger and others that are committing so much senseless violence has never been conditioned to exercise self-restraint. Consequences in most cases are the furthest thing from a thugs mind. They have never been conditioned to expect swift and sure punishment for wrong doing.

As human we all at times get angry and frustrated, but someone with self-restraint don't just fly of the handle. Someone that has been taught self-restraint as a child is highly unlikely to just strike out with senseless violence.

Sure, almost every human being is capable of committing a violent act if provoked enough, but that is not the case with young black males. They are killing each other at the drop of a hat at an alarming rate all over the country.

The culture mentality must be shaped very young then eighteen years later you will have a productive responsible human being; otherwise you will keep producing die hard gang bangers with a destructive mentality. I think one of the biggest problems in the black community is we don't know who our friends are.

In the end no one is going to save the black community except itself. However, it is about control, who exercises control. Anybody getting fed up and wanting to get tough and throw all of drug dealers and bad guys out is going to run up against the system.

This is America we are ruled by law, but that don't mean a community has to roll over and give up. Good and decent people always have the advantage, because at heart all people want to be thought of as good and decent. That is why culture is the most important thing of all for survival.

I don't care if you can't find but one or two decent people in a whole community those two should bond and shun all corruption. That is how decent people get and exercise control in their community, the wheat must be separated from the chaff meaning the good must be separated from the bad or one apple will spoil the whole barrel.

And there should be no exceptions unless one meets the minimum standards. To me it is the dumbest and silliest thing when supposedly intelligent African Americans wonder why taxicabs don't want to stop for blacks and why many people distrust young black males.

Hell, black taxicab drivers don't want to pick up black males, grow up and take responsibility, and I'm going to keep loving all people No matter who hates or disagrees with me. A community must separate itself from the rotten or the whole batch will be tainted in some way that is not just me saying it, that is reality.

All it takes is for decent people to set a standard, bond, and help and support each other, and hang tough. The corrupted must be shunned with no exception, which is not easy to do because everyone no matter how unfit is somebody's son, daughter, brother, sister, mom, dad, aunt, uncle, grandmother, grand dad, etc.

If a high standard is maintained everyone will soon want what you have. But, the system will chew you up and spit you out if there is ever a hint of violence to keep anyone out. The bad guys don't give a damn about obeying any law.

You can't beat them at their game, and they can't beat you at yours if you shun them stick together and stay the course. God save our African American community.

PS: Folks, like I keep repeating, its culture, culture, culture, and more culture, meaning a lack of it. There is no denying the fact proportional wise there is more African Americans babies being killed in the womb than anywhere in the world, Lord help us.

.

I think there is a phenomenon in the human psyche that I'm going to name "The master authority syndrome." I describe it as an awareness of who we perceive to be the master authority in our life. I believe it is something in our human makeup that aids our social survival. I believe nature programmed us to be aware of who is the master authority and to know ones place in the pecking order.

That is my theses, it is not based on any research or anything else, and it's just my wisdom and observation. Now, let's apply it to the African American experience in America. African Americans were brought to America as slaves and stripped bare of their language and culture. Back in slavery from the beginning of the new African American psyche, it was drummed in that the white master authority was the only authority.

From a survival point of view African Americans had to keep aware of the white color of the master authority or be perceived as a threat. So, if a black face is mentally blocked from becoming an authority that locked blacks into a permanent dependent role. And one of the pitfalls of being a dependent is sibling rivalry for the approval of the master authority.

Overall the African Americans psyche and mentality has changed very little since slavery. The African American hue ranges from ebony black to almost Lilly white, but overall we still have a white identity mentality. Subconsciously African Americans still perceive black to be dependent and inferior to the preferred white master authority.

As a race today; we still subconsciously see our black brothers as competitors and the enemy in winning white master authority approval. We won't as a race help or support each other in business if there is a choice. Before the welfare state African Americans were slowly shedding their slavery baggage. Back then an all black neighborhood was the safest place a black person could be, but now it is the most dangerous place a black can be.

Back then blacks were very proud of their neighborhoods, some of the houses were run down but everyone took good care of what they had. Black business men were proud to locate in the black neighborhoods. Now, fast forward to today's African American mentality. If we didn't have a black identity bias why would our educated and elites want to get as far away as they can afford from an all black neighborhood.

Many will say the all black neighborhoods are too crime ridden, that may be true, but, blacks were fleeing well before rampant crime took over, the movie "A raising in the sun" proved that. Every other race will establish upper and middle class zones in and around their own community, why not African Americans? Sure, I may criticize African American rich and elites for deserting the black community, but the real true culprit that have destroyed our community pride and racial self-respect is the welfare state. Enough said, I think you get the point.

I know some may think I'm some kind of black separatist or anti-white hater, but nothing could be further from the truth. In fact I love white people and all people. I don't think Richard M. Nixon was far off the mark with some of the things he said about Africa. African Americans can learn to help and support each other and overcome this vicious sibling rivalry that is killing off so many of our young blacks.
The young African Americans don't know it, but subconsciously they are calling each other nigger and degrading an imaginary black faced rival and enemy that is inferior and doesn't deserve respect. Even though their face is the same color their own desired self image are white. The way out is to learn to love and respect all people. And here is a good formula, just repeat this quote until you learn it by heart. "I can wish all people

goodwill through God which strengthens me."

One will never denigrate his immediate family unless he doesn't feel a part of it. It is the same with ones own race family. One will not denigrate his race by using the hated "N" word unless he mentally doesn't feel part of something dear to him. That is because he doesn't mentally know who he is. But, of course there are a few who are ignorant and just don't give a damn. Also, I don't buy this loony idea that "you take the sting out of a degrading word by excess usage."

For African Americans to help and support each other the surest way would be to have a genuine survival need for each other, but that can't happen as long as we have this handout welfare state. "What the hell needs can a poor black man fill for a woman except stud service and companionship at her whim, when uncle sugar with his food stamps and countless social programs is her real provider and caretaker?"

To prove just how far this society has sunk, ninety five percent of the people in this country will think what I just said was sexist and insane. Only about five percent of the people left in this country will have the wisdom to know that what I just said is defending the nuclear family in the face of government abuse by liberal bleeding heart do-gooders.

Without the strong traditional nuclear family this country can't survive a nuclear blast, an economical collapse, or hardly anything. I double dog dare you! Prove me wrong! We have no bartering capacity left or food supplies on hand over a few days. And attacking me personally will prove nothing.

Unless this welfare state is dismantled and the nuclear family restored along with small farmers and home gardeners, this country and western civilization is doomed. What's going to happen when the dollar becomes worthless? Which won't be very much longer? You know something is terrible, terrible wrong when the rats are already secretly leaving the ship. All of these so called experts, especially women you see on TV with the gift of gab talking only rhetoric, they don't have a clue as to what it will take for this great nation to survive under distress.

In my view the freedom we now enjoy may be down to one decade left. I wouldn't be one bit surprised if within ten years the US will be ruled by some kind of civilian junta, following martial law. There is no doubt in my mind that it is only a matter of time before this big spending welfare state economy collapses. The president and congress should be trying to prepare and save the central government by jettisoning as many of its burdens' as possible. But, instead they are adding more and more big government program burdens.

They should be weaning people off the dole
to prepare them to survive on their own as
much as possible without government.
Believe it or not a survival need is what holds
a society together. The reason the nuclear
family is not supreme anymore is because big
government spending took away the survival
need for it.

Sure, if government start weaning people
there are going to be a lot of hot air and real
suffering and even deaths, but the good will
far out weigh the bad by bringing back the
strong nuclear family savior. That is the only
way the US is going to be able to survive a
nuclear attack or a collapsed economy,
otherwise we can kiss this country goodbye.

When all is said and done, a civilization's
survival depends on its offspring. The only
true guarantee of a nation's survival is its
parents raising responsible children to care
for the parents when they are too old to care
for themselves. There is no getting around
this fact, unless you are one of the few very
rich. The nuclear family is the only system
know to man that can carry out this feat and
guarantee lasting survival.

It seems the only time the people in this
country are going to wake up is when the
checks they receive will hardly buy a loaf of

bread. Them all hell is going to break loose, there will be bottle necks everywhere, there will be rioting in the streets everywhere, and there will be starving and mass killings everywhere. And the masses of hungry undisciplined government dependents are going to feel what's yours is now theirs. The freedoms we now enjoy will be down the tube probably forever. As for me, I just hope I'm wrong on my predictions.

Mean while back to the subject, the only other way African Americans can help and support each other is through individual "Positive thinking." Just memorize the following quote and repeat it to yourself often, "I can wish all people goodwill through God which strengthens me." The answer to why African Americans vote overwhelming for one party has to do with a dependent mentality.

A parent can be a scheming phony, a two faced liars, and even worse, but as long as the kid (African America) is fed and not overly abused the kid is going to support that parent regardless. African Americans somewhere along the line perceived the democrat party as their white master authority parent.

It is like the unconditional love a mother has for her child. And the welfare state guarantees that African Americans and the poor stays dependent minded, thereby creating an emotional bond that cannot be broken, until these dependents are forced to grow up, stand on their own and make adult responsible choices.

Lately I hear the term "Protect the Children" and we know what is best for the children. In my view it is like "The blind men examining an elephant." I can't remember all of the details, but all three came away with a different conclusion, one thought the legs were tree trunks. From a big picture point of view it is impossible for the welfare state to truly protect the children. 6 November 2011, late injection: Click > the blind men and the Elephant.

Until recently, going back over five thousand years the children were always protected because of one simple fact, the parents needed them for survival. Today most parents see children as love items to be pampered and doted upon. Kids are almost never seen as future meal tickets, which they are. The welfare state has taken away the need for the male head of household and the need to raise children like ones life will depends on it.

The supreme natural law of human survival is based on a survival need, and bleeding heart do good liberals have all but destroyed any need for responsibility, accountability, or anything else. I'm totally against any abuse of any child for any reason, period. God save us.

The old Du bois versus Booker T. Washington two schools of thought still haven't been settled and probably never will. Washington believed that African Americans should take the self reliance route and focus first on learning the basic trade vocations to feed and control their own destiny. He didn't put a priority on integration.

On the other hand, Du bois disagreed openly with Washington and believed that African Americans should not be limited in anyway. Du bois believed that blacks should go the full integration route and focus on the best education possibly. In my view the Du bois way was the right way in theory and it won out on the course blacks should take even to today.

But, as any scientist will tell you what works in theory doesn't necessarily work in practice. In almost all cases for any race to improve overall it must be pulled up from the top because those are the ones with the education and resources to make it happen. For many races there are no color differences, that way they can blend in and move into the mainstream very easily, no problem.

But, for African Americans the norm doesn't work in practice. The two main drawbacks are color difference and African American culture. In my view the biggest failure to uplift African Americans have been the black elite by deserting the black community. Sure, crime and drugs are the excuse now, but that started long before crime and drugs were a big problem; just remember the movie "A raising in the sun."

I understand safety and the need for a pecking order, but blacks could establish middle and upper class zones in or on the edge of black communities if they wanted to. Also, blacks should open businesses and invest back in their own communities like all other races, but it's not happening on a large scale. I think It's something a lot deeper here that African Americans need to face and accept.

I think African Americans as a race are still running away from themselves and their communities. I don't think African Americans as a whole respect themselves unconditional as individuals and as a race with all the flaws and blemishes, unconditionally. I don't think most blacks have a do-for-your-self independent mentality that will make you respect yourself and people that look like you.

I think we as blacks need to face and accept one another with pride and nothing to prove, flawed and scarred but as good as anybody or any race, period. "We don't need a ticket to ride, or to qualify, no one asked to be born, just forgive and accept the past and move on." Do-for-your-self people don't worry about imaginary threats from the past or empty symbolisms; they are too busy working to live a proud independent dignified life.

No one can truly accept and respect you unless you first accept and respect yourself, unconditionally. The color different won't let blacks just blend into the mainstream unnoticed, plus, there is an unspoken negative stereotypical image of blacks as a whole. That unspoken image associates blacks as a whole with property devalue, social baggage, crime, and a few other negative stereotypes.

Still, genes are getting through because in my view big booties are no longer limited to African Americans. The culture drawback is far too many African Americans still unconsciously believe the old black stereotype that black is inferior (that the white man's beer is colder). Far too many blacks still see other blacks as competitors and the enemy in winning mainstream approval.

For that reason we tend not to support one another as a whole in business in the black communities like back in the nineteen forties and fifties.

Lately I hear the term "Protect the Children" and we know what is best for the children. In my view it is like "The three blind men examining an elephant." I can't remember all of the details, but all three came away with a different conclusion, one thought the legs were tree trunks. From a big picture point of view it is impossible for the welfare state to truly protect the children.

Until recently, going back over five thousand years the children were always protected because of one simple fact, the parents needed them for survival. Today most parents see children as love items to be pampered and doted upon. Kids are almost never seen as future meal tickets, which they are. The welfare state has taken away the need for the male head of household and the need to raise children like ones life will depends on it.
The supreme natural law of human survival is based on a survival need, and bleeding heart do good liberals have all but destroyed any need for responsibility, accountability, or anything else. I'm totally against any abuse of any child for any reason, period. God save

us.

Well, for what it is worth I decided to add my two cents to the subject, "On the down low." It is no secret that AIDS is far out of proportion in the African American communities and even on Historically Black Colleges and Universities (HBCUs). There must be a reason why this is so. I was the first one that pointed out that the revolving door in and out of the prison system was the leading factor. But, that still doesn't explain why this out of proportion also exists on HBCUs.

That means there must be a culture factor involved. Many believe it is how the African American community defines homosexuality. The general mainstream assumption is that anyone participating in a homosexual act is a homosexual, but that is not what many minority men believe. A great many minority men view homosexuality basically in the same light as masturbation. They view the act in terms of dominant or submission or driver or receiver.

They believe that as long as they are in the dominant role and doing the driving their manhood is not at issue or threatened. They feel they are only acting like a squirrel as long as it is kept secret. Whereas, it is only the one that is in the submissive and receiving role that makes one a homosexual. As a writer I'm not deciding anything, I'm just trying to shine as much light as possible on the true mindset.

To get at the AIDS problem, you first need to understand what people are really thinking. The fact is, it boils down to the same old saw, that is permissive sexual behavior and loose morals. Men have in the past and will always try to get easy sex from whoever will give it up. So, the ultimate AIDS solution lies with the women in this country. Women need to stop giving up all of this easy unobligated sex, period. And I put the entire blame on why they won't keep their legs cross on the welfare state.

Before the welfare state a woman needed and depended on men for survival and there was no way most was going to give up their number one bargaining chip without a commitment of some sort

Back before we had a super big government sugar daddy provider, very few African American women would give up easy sex without an obligated commitment, and even then he had to be of sound character. Back then If a suitor wouldn't go to church and clean up his act, it was "Her way or the highway," and she had a strong dad or brother that would kick butt to back her up. My solution as always gets the government the hell out of the family provider business.

In my opinion, AIDS in the African American community is approaching the out of control level. Now because of the vast improvement of new drug we don't hear much about AIDS anymore but still that don't mean it's gone away. There is still no cure and taking what is called a cocktail of drugs is no easy burden on the stomach.

The subject of prostitution is where you will find more hypocrites and self-righteousness than anywhere else. I'm not condoning anything, I'm just writing my views and observations. When you go back in history one thing all civilizations had in common was they had the wisdom to leave certain things alone. Prostitution was one of those things. It has always been legal and tolerated throughout history for a very good reason.

In fact, in my view it is shallow and stupid to make prostitution illegal, why do you think we have so many child molesters and all kinds of perverts? Sure, regulate it and keep it under control but it should never be made illegal. Mother Nature gave great pleasure to eating and sex to make sure there will be future generations. Therefore, those with real wisdom tend to leave prostitution alone as a necessary sin and not preach and fool around with it.

Prostitution is a venting mechanism that takes pressure off the good decent nuclear family way of life. There are certain things we can pretend to get rid of, but in reality we can't and still remain civilized. We may be human, civilized, and all that, but we still have animal instincts. Right now, there is more sneaking around after dark than most of us would like to believe. Sexual energy is no fantasy it is physical and real whether we like it or not.

It is one of the most powerful forces in our entire make up. Sexual energy will build up like pressure in a steel drum and if it is not vented in a harmless way society is going to pay a price. It's not something that can be snuffed out without serious side effects; sages of the distance past understood that. Just look around to where the force of some of this energy is popping out in perverted ways. There is a reason why the world's oldest profession is still around.

Many will strongly disagree with my observations on this, but in my view the oldest profession has always been and will always be a societal relief valve. It is a relief valve for the unmarried and many other situations. Common sense should tell you what happens when a relief valve is closed off, something is gonna blow. Men by nature are aggressive creatures and sometimes one slight touch or one show of affection will prevent total self-destruction.

As it is those that are ugly, antisocial, and with many other imperfections can't find legal sexual relief. Most men can channel their sexual energy into other productive things, but some cannot. Why do you think we have such a long list of child molesters and other perverts now days? My guess is un-vented sexual energy is one leading cause. With no legal relief of sexual energy the only choice for many is manual self-relief (with the aid of porn).

To get sexual relief a lot of men have sold out their soul and true beliefs, then start believing their sold out views as fact, that is one reason why you see so many spineless men today. Most of us have seen cases where a young man stays in trouble and is out of control, and then he finds a girl friend or gets married and becomes as calm as a cucumber. Sure, he may feel more responsible, but the main reason is most of his aggression is being vented.

Capitalizing on self-sexual relief is what's behind and driving this whole out of control invasive video pornography sex industry. There may be a lot of lookers, but the ones actually spending big money and buying are viewing for masturbating purpose, which is supporting and allowing all of this sluttish invasive stuff to be in our face. Why would one pay to watch a video when they can legal get the real thing?

Sure, a few might but I don't believe the big bucks would be driving it like what is happening now. Surprisingly, women make up almost half of these buying consumers (which may include a bathroom ceremony complete with candles).

Come on folks! Far too many men are watching porn, and what woman ain't got a hidden toy, give me a break, who knows, maybe it's just me imagining too many things, maybe I should admit publishing this whole article was a gross mistake and pretend it never happened. Forgive my bad judgment folks, lesson learned.

However, I got news for anyone watching too much pornography. It can dull ones sexual imagination and lock one into a visual stimulation only mode in order to stay aroused. And make even a teenager addictive to where normal sex is not possible. My intent is not to write how thing should or should not be, but to write things the way they really are.
So, "How do you like me now?

This subject reminds me of the vacationing

tourist that walked up to a local that had his feet propped up and was kicked back under a tree. The tourist asked the man, "Why don't you get up and get a job?" The local said, "For what?" "To make money." "Make money for what," said the local? "So you can relax, enjoy yourself, and take it easy later in life."

The local said, "Why bother I'm already doing all that." The point I'm trying to make is what really matters in life is food, shelter, and the basics for a comfortable life. It matters not if one makes a hundred dollars a day if one can't afford enough food, shelter, warmest, and the basic comforts of life.

In my view protecting the culture and producing enough food to survive should always be the first priorities for any country. The surest way to destroy any country is to take away its struggle to survive, period. When the struggle to survive goes, so goes individual accountability and responsibility followed by disrespect for authority, moral decay, crime, drug, and on and on.

In my view any poor country that has great wealth in natural resources or by any other means should use a dual track economy. What I mean by dual track is always keep the great wealth income completely separated to be spent only on infra structural, and never to be use for handouts. In fact stay away from hand outs, period, if you want to save your culture, handouts is a white man's disease.

I don't believe there is a poor country anywhere that couldn't feed itself on its own if the government would allow producers to keep ninety percent of all profit. There would be entrepreneurs springing up almost overnight to fill the need, but those governments would never keep hand off higher taxes, no way.

The other day I was listening to this commentator and he asked something to this effect, "Can you prove that we are not the most intelligent beings in the universe." I thought about that and decided to ponder the question. I'm not sure if I or anyone can prove it but I know there is a higher power, you can call him God, Jehovah, Allah, A superior being, or whatever. You see, we are in a mental box called logic.

We are locked in and cannot escape. With only logic we will never be able to understand the beginning of our existence or our purpose here on earth. Logic dictates that there had to be a beginning at some point in time, which makes it impossible to ever understand our existence with only logic. The actual facts are man doesn't truly know what time or existence mean. Example: Computers are locked in a binary system and cannot escape.

Computers respond only to a negative or a positive polarity. Super computers are super fast but they still can't get past the binary system. Our five senses connects us to reality, otherwise there would be no reality. Does that mean there would still be reality if no life could sense it? Like the old question: "If a tree fell in the Forrest and there were nothing or no body there to hear it, would there be a sound?"

Who knows, in time other senses could evolve to produce a higher level of intelligent. There are animals that have senses that can match almost anything we can do with modern technology and probably countless other things we haven't discovered and are not aware of. There are animals that have senses of radar, sonar, electricity, and many other things that modern technology can and cannot do.

Who knows, there may be infinite worlds and dimensions coexisting with us that we don't have the senses to detect. Who knows how Nessie and Bigfoot come and goes. In most of the animal world smell is the dominant sense and is many, many times more powerful than ours. Down wind a polar bear can smell prey almost a hundred miles away. It is almost unbelievable what a blood hound can do with the sense of smell.

Logic dictates that there must be a beginning to everything. Just think of the old riddle, "Which came first, the chicken or the egg?" Being boxed in with logic we can't even solve a simple little riddle like that. But, we know the answer must lie somewhere. We understand relativity; nothing doesn't just happen with no connection. In closing, wise men realized long ago that our power to reason was limited, so for the sake of sanity there must be a deity or deities with all the answers.

I totally agree. Wait, hold on a moment, I've decided to delve deeper into this chicken and egg riddle. Actually there is no such thing as which came first in the "Which came first, the chicken or the egg riddle." The chicken or the egg riddle is actually a life cycle circuit which is a unit of one. No matter how many parts a circuit has it still operates as one unit. My observation of the unit of one oneness opens up far deeper questions, but I will leave it there for now.

Sure, life can evolve and adapt, but, a beginning life cycle circuit must be made, powered, maintained, and exist for some purpose. We humans don't make electrical circuits without some purpose.

THE END

To Purchase:
Freddie L. Sirmans, Sr. Books:
Website: www.FLSirmans.com